CLAIRVOYANCE:

Reweaving the Fabric of Community for Black Folk

CLAIRVOYANCE:

Reweaving the Fabric of Community for Black Folk

Prepared Jointly by

Associated Black Charities
Coppin State College
Morgan State University

Edited by

John H. Morris, Jr.
Charles G. Tildon, Jr.

NEW THINKING PUBLICATIONS
Baltimore, Maryland

NEW THINKING PUBLICATIONS
Baltimore, Maryland

Library of Congress Catalogue
Card Number: 98-84559

ISBN 0-9663205-0-6

Manufactured in the United States of America
Printed by BCP Digital Printing, Baltimore, Maryland

Additional text editing by Noni Faruq

We wish to thank and acknowledge the many people who contributed to this book by participating in the various New Thinking Forums, the various working meetings that arose from New Thinking, or anyone who shared with us an honest appraisal of where things stood. You know who you are.

This book is for anyone who has looked around, in bemusement, at a world you did not make, recognizing that you saw things differently than those around you. You know who you are, who at the moment of your greatest frustration could only ask the question: "Hey, is it me — or what?"

Table of Contents

INTRODUCTION:
The Point of a Policy for Us by Us

No policy can serve well two masters. If those who crafted the policy are not those it was intended to benefit, the policy will serve the interests of one group more than the other. Despite everyone's good intentions, the policy inevitably will benefit the people who made it more than those for whom it was said to be made.

For too long, we African Americans have been the prisoners of the categories of someone else's thinking. We not only need to find our own voice. We must divine our own syntax to express and describe the world, as we see it and would see it if we could just reform it, for our own purpose.

For too long, public policy has been intended to benefit the interests of a population that happened just to include African Americans. That policy though was not crafted by African Americans. Its assumptions were not the assumptions of African Americans. The strategies it implied were not the strategies of African Americans. It is not, therefore, surprising that the benefits of that policy crafted by others have not well served the interests of African Americans.

These thoughts are intended to embody new thinking on public policy, if only because it is thinking on public policy for African Americans by African Americans. The product of that thinking should have an application beyond the parochial interests of Black folk. Looking clearly at a subject unashamedly from a

1

vantage different from one we are used to might just produce a few good ideas we all could use.

We have proceeded to look at the future as African Americans unburdened by the realities of the present and elevated by an understanding of ourselves that assumes our worth. It is one thing to "say it loud . . . ." It is quite another to craft from that premise a thoughtful and coherent public policy. That is our aim.

Making policy by being who we are changes what policy making means. It no longer serves as the exclusive province of the politically connected, the financially well off, or the academically tutored. Policy making can serve the needs of everyday people by opening policy making to all of us.

When all of us make policy, that circumstance alone changes the world we know into the world we make. We no longer exist as bystanders in communities that others allow us to occupy. We become owners of the communities we make.

We need only know who we are, what we want, and be prepared to do what is necessary to make the world truly our own. With that resolve, policy making becomes an assertion of identity.

By making policy, we define not who we are but who we want to become. If we want to become people of value, whose independence and autonomy shapes limitless possibilities for us, then only we can shape the policy that makes those possibilities our reality.

We cannot become what we choose unless we say so by the policy choices we make for ourselves. For us to make those choices, we must bring policy making to the grassroots -- from the boardroom to the barbershop. This is the objective of New Thinking.

To capture the idea of who we can be, we have created our future in the transformed landscape of a rejuvenated city and in the person of a remarkable, though otherwise ordinary, woman, Sylvia Forrest. That city and that woman are fictional. They also happen to be real.

Sylvia Forrest arose out of frustration, anger, and resentment. That is simply to say that she is African American. She lives to transcend and transform those feelings into something she can use. That is just to say that she is a woman who has taken charge of her own destiny to make it what she needs it to be.

In reaching for more than she can have despite her awareness of all that would be denied her, she could be a heroic, tragic or even comic figure -- or maybe all of these at once. Whichever, it remains for us to judge.

We often ignore the reality that, for many African Americans, to be alive, awake and aware is to risk insanity. For those of us exiled here on the North American continent, the world makes no sense. What we see just makes us crazy -- or so others tell us.

Each day we are compelled to live out the curse of Tantalus. In myth, Tantalus was condemned to stand eternally in water he could never manage to drink and to see beautiful boughs of fruit always just beyond his reach whenever he tried to eat.

Like Tantalus, we African Americans see arrayed before us all the good things we see others relish. These things tempt us greatly. We reach out to grab even a small share of the plenty around us. Then, by some magic we can never understand, hidden hands snatch this sweet fruit from us or some malignant breeze causes the feast we would enjoy to rot in our mouths just after we begin to savor its delicate taste.

What options then do we have if we have to live as Tantalus? We can dull our minds to the reality of our predicament and pretend to enjoy a feast we never get to eat. We can reject the feast altogether and savor the starvation that may be the only thing that is ours to own. Thus, the ultimate resolution for us is self-consuming ignorance, self-deceiving illusion, or self-destroying despair.

As we look at the condition of African Americans years after the unfulfilled promise of equal opportunity, we see the lingering effects of our peculiar dilemma. We also can see in that predicament a bond that ties all of us who share this continent and trace our roots back to Africa.

We can understand the isolation of those who go through the motions, pretending to enjoy a feast they can never have. Whether they live in wonderful homes in tree-lined suburbs or work in marvelous glass towers teeming with people in business suits carrying brief cases, they share two truths that join them with the rest of us -- in our shared unhappiness.

First, they likely are alone where they are. The wonder of their existence is not broad enough to admit more than a few like us. The illusion of their affluence is precarious. They always face the risk of being expelled from their perceived paradise.

Second, despite their rarity and despite whatever talent that may have placed them where they are, they will never progress to the level of their talent while they see others unlike them progress far beyond the limits of their capabilities. Only in their isolation from the rest of us can they support the illusion of their lives. Only then can they hide the pain of the insanity they are forced to live.

We can also feel the misery of those who would choose to starve in the midst of plenty. Choosing nothing from this elusive feast is the only real power you can wield if you happen to be Tantalus.

Look at those of us trapped in a poverty that extends generations into the past. Or, see those who choose each morning to sleep in yet another day rather than seek out a fortune that always manages to escape us.

We share the same fate as those of us who faithfully commute each day to the frustration of an office existence that leads to nowhere in particular. We are all Tantalus. We just deal differently -- each as Tantalus nonetheless.

Sylvia Forrest, however, rejected that destiny. She refused to partake of the feast. She also refused to starve. Last, she refused to pretend she did not see.

She chose, instead, to see differently. In the world she saw, there was no cruel destiny. In the world she saw, she was not Tantalus. She was Midas.

In her world, Midas was not the greedy king of myth who was trapped and ultimately cursed by his avarice into wishing that everything he touched would turn to gold. Sylvia transformed the myth. In her version, Midas was a magician who freed his world from the curse of having nothing by making the everyday valuable.

Her slant on the Midas myth is our way out of the Tantalus circle. We do not have to be denied forever someone else's feast.

CLAIRVOYANCE

We can make our own feast of what we already have. If we have nothing, we then can make nothing valuable.

Sylvia Forrest is a powerful woman. She is powerful not because she was born to wealth. She was born a public housing tenant. She is powerful not because she was elected to high office. She sought no office of power. She is powerful not because she had extraordinary learning. She barely finished high school and never completed college.

She is powerful for just one reason. She has imagination. She can see what is not there and make it happen because she sees it.

Policy making is little more than describing the world as we would like it to be just to make it so. To make that world become real, we must first see it and then help others like us to see it too -- for themselves.

This, too, was Sylvia's challenge -- to show her family, friends, and neighbors the nearness of new possibilities for themselves. By seeing a world of new possibilities, together they can then make a new world possible.

These are the people who change the world. Sylvia Forrest happens to be one of them. She also happens to be African American. For us to change our world for our own purpose, we, too, must be Sylvia.

Her story is about the power of imagination to reshape the world -- if only to change what it looks like in our minds. For those people who do change the world, changing how we see the world is enough to change it. Whatever we then do after that necessarily and forever changes the way things are.

INTRODUCTION

For us, the instrument of our imagination is New Thinking. It seeks to change the outcomes of our lives by changing how we, and those around us, think in the world we would master for ourselves and for our purposes.

For us, the point of policy making by us and for us is to create new myths that make the world work for us. Such policy making means more than writing legislation, pursuing litigation, and holding policy forums. We have been doing all of these things for years with little effect.

Our challenge is, instead, to spark and capture the imagination of Black folk to see the world anew -- to see a world that serves our interests for our purposes to our benefit. Our challenge then is to reinvent what we now see as our world. In the discussions that follow, we seek to do just that by the questions and the explorations that we call "New Thinking."

An Overview of New Thinking

This "New Thinking" Project began with several simple assumptions. The assumptions grew into bold assertions. The bold assertions reshaped how we saw ourselves and thought about the world.

The boldest of these assumptions was a future that worked for people like us. It was just up to us to define it for ourselves. That future could only exist if we defined it and refused to let anyone else define it for us.

It occurred to us that we had forgotten how to see as Africans. After hundreds of years sharing the North American continent with others from all over the world, we had learned much of how others see. We saw as America's orphans, assimilated to a family that was not ours and never would be. We saw as outsiders striving to belong where we were not wanted.

Still, we had not reclaimed what we had lost arriving upon these shores: the ability to see a world made for us. We had forgotten to see with the confident belief that we belonged where we were and where we were belonged to us.

More than anything else, we forgot the simple truth that we belonged to ourselves and to one another. Defeated by the reality of our present predicament, we had lost our vision of our own prosperity -- together as a people not alone as individuals.

We began this project as African Americans long tired of seeing ourselves and our world through someone else's eyes. We were too much immersed in ideas about us that made us somebody else's problem to solve, somebody else's illness to cure, or the object of somebody else's charity to support. If we were to reclaim ourselves as a prosperous people, we had to see differently.

It occurred to us that the world that had oppressed us sorely was the product of assumptions chosen by everyone else -- but us. To find again the confidence we once had of who we were, we had to reinvent the world -- from assumptions that we chose for ourselves.

We began that reinvention with a joint undertaking. We gathered as African Americans to think about ourselves and the world differently. We met to do this new thinking differently. The least of the products of our effort may be these writings that came out of our meetings.

Our most satisfying accomplishment was, however, the process around which we came together as a body of trusting people -- not an assembly of self-interested individuals. In that process, we rediscovered the Africans we once were. We saw a new reality for us in which together each of us was better than any one of us could have been alone.

The Beginning of New Thinking

We began our new thinking several years ago. We decided to come together as African Americans to think and talk together.

Together, we were then free to say the things each of us had pondered in our enforced isolation from one another. Together, we could share intimately the thoughts that seemed only to emerge from others like us.

We had just four rules:

1. Leave your egos at the door;
2. Leave your agendas at the door;
3. Confidentiality is sacrosanct; and
4. Be prepared to challenge your own assumptions.

What emerged from these meetings was a consistent point of view about things that was uniquely our own. We were a diverse group in vocation, personality, temperament, and age. We were all, however, African American.

While we did not agree, we came to understand the interests around which we inevitably came together. That understanding of interests formed the point of view that was ours and ours alone. Thus began our rediscovery of what we had lost in North America.

We talked. We disagreed. We probed and challenged one another. We questioned established ideas. Last, we dreamed what we wanted from the world. Yet, most important, we trusted one another.

What came out of our shared deliberations was different from what each of us had been led to "know" by others. It embraced what each of us had always known alone, enhanced and elevated by what we then discovered together: that together we could know more than we could apart.

The Expansion of New Thinking

We then looked to apply our discovery about ourselves to reshape how we viewed the world around us. We expanded our small circle to include a larger number of African Americans focusing on discrete aspects of life in our communities.

Our effort encompassed six forums to which we planned to invite others to join us in New Thinking. We set about to examine issues in the following areas: housing, economic development, education, health care, transportation, and raising the next generation.

As we prepared for these New Thinking discussions, we carefully considered who to invite and how to structure the discussions to embrace the experiences that we had had with one another. We looked for two types of people to be included: (1) creative thinkers generally interested in any subject affecting African Americans; and (2) people with special expertise to contribute on the various subjects for discussion.

The model for our deliberations was not the symposium on a learned subject. We did not see ourselves as scholars pursuing some proposition of specialized knowledge. Rather, we were more like home owners seeking to discern for ourselves how we wanted our house to appear. We were the owners deciding what features we wanted in the house -- not the architects who would be hired to satisfy those specifications.

In selecting the people who would join us in New Thinking, we focused more on who could live within our four rules than on expertise. As we pondered this person and that, the controlling consideration was how the person would affect the group in its discussions and less on the special knowledge or information the individual might possess.

Each discussion began with the same general question: in our consideration of these various issues as African Americans, what do we want? When the issue was housing, our starting question was *"To create the kind of community that I would want to live in, what kind of housing environment and what kind of housing must we have, and what must housing policy be to achieve that community?"* The question remained the same, though the focus shifted to the kind of economy our community needed, the education the economy required, and the health care that all of us wanted.

We began our deliberations with groups of anywhere from 25-to-35 people. Initially, we explored our underlying assumptions, the limitations our current predicament imposed, and the ultimate objective we all agreed was desired.

Having agreed about where we wanted to go, the sessions split into more intimate discussions of more focused topics to give our vision of the desired community greater substance. These topics included such questions as

- Do our present housing and community design assumptions work for African Americans? How should these assumptions be changed? What does such design change produce?
- Where does the money come from for people to have the kind of housing I would want for myself?
- What must we do now to develop in people a common caring and purpose to bring African Americans together, living and working productively to create a healthy housing environment?
- To have the kind of housing environment that I would want for myself as an African American, what must the demographics of the environment be? Who must be part of the community? How different are these demographics from present trends? What demographic factors should housing policy take into account to promote a desirable housing environment?
- To get to a prosperous future from a present not so prosperous, African Americans have to find and develop assets most people now overlook. Assuming a prosperous future long-term, how do we begin the journey today to that future? How do we create the value today that produces the wealth we need tomorrow?
- What must we do now to develop, in people who may mistrust the idea of economic progress, a sense of common purpose to bring African Americans together,

working productively to create unknown prosperity for ourselves?

- To have the kind of economy that works for people like us, what kinds of human assets does this economy require? What skills need the people have? Where do they get the skills? What sort of things do we need to have these people doing? What kinds of backgrounds does this economy require? How do we get the people we need for the economy to work to engage in the economy?

- What do we want education to be like in our community? What should it do? What is its place and role in a world that works for people like us?

- How do we go about educating to assure that people know what they must for our community to succeed?

- What benchmarks of educational progress are meaningful for us?

- What does a health care system that works for African Americans provide to meet the health care needs of African Americans?

- How should African Americans go about securing the resources to meet our health care needs?

- How do we deliver health care services so that the health care needs of African Americans are taken care of? What should the structure look like to meet the community's health care needs? What are the services? Who provides them? Where do the service providers come from? How do we identify the service recipients? How do we reach the service recipients? Who pays for the services? How do they pay?

- To have the kind of health care that works for people like us, what kinds of human assets does this health care framework require -- in service providers, underwriters, and consumers? What skills need the people have? Where do they get the skills? What sort of things do we need to have these people doing? What kinds of backgrounds does this health care require? How do we get the people we need for health care to work to engage in the objectives of health?

After meeting together separately on these various subjects, the New Thinking group reassembled to draw more generalized conclusions. With these conclusions, we began to weave a tapestry of community for African Americans that in many important respects looked different from the view that others held for us.

A New Tapestry of Community

We came together around a notion of community that emerged from our disparate discussions. From our assumptions, we offered the following insights about a prosperous future for African Americans:

On Housing:

- Black folk have to *own* their own communities.
- We must offer real choice.
- We cannot plan to save all Black people.
- The point of housing is to build community.
- Community and identity are related. *Community* is where all of us look to define who we are as African Americans, personally, economically or otherwise. It is our home base.
- We cannot have the community we need without a strong economic base to make our choices real. ***Housing policy cannot exist without economic development.***
- We cannot build the community we need without a base of values that allows community to exist.
- To achieve our policy objectives, we need
  - ‣ Economic integration, not necessarily racial integration
  - ‣ Housing stock that can be developed as people progress economically rather than disposed of
  - ‣ Proximity to the amenities of community: a marketplace, good schools, and support services for economic development
  - ‣ Commercial integration with housing.

On Economic Development:

- Economic development means creating African American wealth.
- Our focus is on *ownership*:
  - ▸ Business before jobs -- to secure employment
  - ▸ Profits over salary -- to progress economically
  - ▸ Equity over debt -- to achieve growth
  - ▸ Investment over saving -- to secure for us the full return
  - ▸ Saving before spending -- to build our dollars
  - ▸ Spending with us -- to keep our dollars with us.
- Not every African American will be wealthy, but all must support the general wealth of African Americans -- all parts of our community are economically allied.
- Economic development requires an uncompromising commitment to excellence. We cannot tolerate mediocrity.
- Economic development that benefits Black folk must have an African American focus, even to the point of appearing separatist. Our communities form our market, our work force, our entrepreneur base, and our resource base. We must protect our base so that we benefit from it fully.
- The focus of an African American economy is entrepreneurial, with a larger concentration of small, micro, or home businesses.

- Information and ideas form our greatest economic resource and the basis of the future economy -- *education is more than training to do business, it is developing the principal resource of our economy.*

On Education:

- The importance of learning to the community is too great to be left to teachers and administrators. It is a challenge that the entire community must embrace directly.
- The community must own, and take ownership in, the teaching of its children.
- We must expand the places where learning occurs to include all those places, formal and informal, where information, values, and training are imparted. We must create in the community "venues for learning" beyond the school room doors.
- Learning for us must embrace the following values:
  - caring
  - discipline
  - exploration
  - a sense of understanding
  - a sense of reward
  - a sense of wonder
  - critical thinking
  - knowledge

CLAIRVOYANCE

- The things we need our children to learn must include the following:
  - reading/communication
  - analytic thinking with words and ideas
  - quantitative thinking with numbers and related concepts
  - negotiation skills
  - research/information development skills
  - creativity
  - peer resistance/influence
  - group living
  - an understanding of success for our own purposes
  - decision-making
  - option creation
  - conflict resolution
  - leadership/followership
- Beyond developing these skills and attributes, our new community will need to support the following values:
  - identity and pride
  - power/mastery/creativity
  - judgment
  - cooperation/power
  - self-actualization
  - autonomy
  - choice
  - hope
  - self-esteem

- As children find more opportunities to learn outside school than within, the community should direct its resources more to make those outside school opportunities more productive.
- The "education system" is not limited to the structures of public education, but embraces all the community's institutions, including its institutions of higher education, its businesses, its civic organizations, and its places of worship, to create a true "community of learning."
- The benchmarks of educational progress within the community ultimately rest in the sound health of the community. A sound system of learning within the community produces people who can achieve success, however they define it. Such a benchmark does not require us to consider such traditional statistics as SAT scores, standardized test results, or dropout rates viewed in isolation of anything else. The objective is not to improve the students' test scores but to nurture productive people.

On Health Care

- The point of health is to feel good and not just to get by, not feeling bad.
- Health for African Americans must make us whole and well without subjecting us to the infirmity of dependence upon the care giver.

- The principal focus of a health care solution that works for African Americans must be based on the goal of preventing infirmity rather than treating or relieving suffering. The desired outcome is to empower people to heal themselves -- or at least to maintain control of their own health care solutions.
- Health care solutions supporting the independence of Black folk will compel the following policy shifts:
  - ▸ Refocusing health care resources from treating and relieving suffering to preventing the ailment that causes it
  - ▸ Rethinking the financing structure to support a disease-prevention-based model
  - ▸ Reshaping our notions of compassion to view differently both present day choices to live a life of excess and waste that lead to future suffering and the present day suffering resulting from the past unwise decisions that people freely made for themselves
  - ▸ Accepting a structure created by, maintained by, and benefitting principally the health care and other interests of African Americans
  - ▸ Recognizing that African American "ownership" of the health care structure is a health issue, not just a matter of fairness or economics.
- The controlling framework is not a hospital model. It is a community model that requires the involvement of an entire community to finance the framework, to empower

those within it to generate the values that make it work, and to provide the structure that accords the care to make people healthy.

The Overview: *On to a Larger Vision*

Whether or not we have discerned new solutions, or even the right solutions, is less important than the fact that we have engaged one another to define our own futures for ourselves. We have begun a process of thinking that binds without requiring regimentation of thought.

We have discovered again new values of cooperation that harken back to our African roots in ways that lead us to a new vision of the future as ourselves: the Africans who have found themselves on the North American continent.

Our thinking began with the first of this collection of thoughts from a perspective that is our own. **Confronting the Arrogance of Dominance** gives the conceptual framework that sparked us initially. It offers the paradoxical reality that only I can make me the equal of anyone. It also follows that I cannot then be free, unless I am free to define who I am and what I would choose for myself.

Our first effort at new thinking on housing produced *Seeing Clearly Housing Options*. The focus of its approach is the necessity of choice to make community for African Americans possible.

The second of these installments, on economic development, is **The Wealth of Black Folk**. It provides a vision of

African American economy borne ultimately upon the talents of those people whose ingenuity and perseverance had maintained us on this continent for hundreds of years. It translates those qualities into new possibilities for the 21st century.

The third of the installments, on education, is **The Fire That Does Not Consume: *New Thinking on Education*.** It offers a community-focused vision of learning in a community consumed with developing the one resource that is undeniable and always renewable: its own knowledge.

The fourth of the installments further refines the vision of education. It is **Finding Ourselves in the Child**. It completes the education vision of a community that renews itself by its effort to restore its children.

The fifth installment addresses the subject of health care for African Americans. It is **Connectedness: *A Prescription for Living Well*.** It presents the vision of a health care framework based upon true *ownership* of the structure to empower African Americans to heal themselves.

Each of these installments conveys its vision of a prosperous future for African Americans. That vision is depicted through the fictional world of Sylvia Forrest, a 21st century inhabitant of a very changed community on the site now occupied by the Lexington Terrace public housing community in Baltimore City.

Through her own courage and confidence, Sylvia has helped reshape the possibilities for people like herself. The ideas that emerged from the New Thinking sessions find their best articulation in Sylvia's story.

CLAIRVOYANCE

"We are all just prisoners here of our own device."
The Eagles, Hotel California, 1976.

Confronting the

ARROGANCE OF

DOMINANCE:

Or Why Equality Cannot Be the Dying Thought of the Powerless

by
John H. Morris, Jr.

I. Introduction

It is the arrogance of Dominance to take itself for granted. Dominance sees through a lens that changes all it sees. It is the arrogance of Dominance to insist that it sees without distortion.

This paper considers how Dominance dictates what equality and diversity mean. From the vantage of Dominance, equality and diversity mean something very different from what these ideas might convey in a world without Dominance. The arrogance of Dominance lies in its casual assumption that no other view is worth considering: the implied and sometime explicit assertion "my way or the highway."

When people begin to choose the "highway," Dominance no longer works to describe the world. If we understand equality and diversity from the assumptions of Dominance, then our understanding, too, loses any meaning connected to the world that is becoming *without* Dominance.

Any law that depends upon that understanding has no place in the changing world. At best, the law becomes irrelevant to times that have moved beyond its assumptions. Where its assumptions are hostile to those of a changing world, the law just gets in the way.

Law ceases to work as law. It can no longer bring order and peace through the myth of justice.

A. The Paradox of Equality

Equality is a gift that cannot be given. As much as you may want for me to have it, giving undoes the gift. If you can give me equality, then we cannot be equal. Equality is a paradox.

Equality is a gift that only I can give to myself. In this sense, the realization of equality is not your relation to me in brotherhood, but my relation to myself in power: the reality of my capacity to shape my own future.

From its vantage, Dominance colors equality with the tint of a brotherhood that focuses upon the intent of those who, like it, act toward me. For Dominance, equality and brotherhood are one.

For me, equality means empowerment. To Dominance, the test of equality is others' goodwill toward me. To me, the test is my ability to realize for myself my own dreams.

B. The Arrogance of Dominance and Equal Protection

We have failed to confront the implication of dominance in the law of equality or equal protection. The law has assumed that, in our social relationships, we are equal. Any existing inequality then must flow from discrimination by people of ill will or bad character. The law, therefore, forbids discrimination and asserts that equal protection of the law means treating everyone the same.

What if inequality were broader than deliberately favoring or disfavoring one group over another? What if our underlying social relationships were inherently unequal, rather than inherently equal? What if everyone were not the same, just different?

We will not, therefore, promote equality just by eliminating discrimination. If we are different, we cannot treat everyone the same without necessarily treating someone unequally.

It is the arrogance of Dominance to ignore difference. Dominance views the world as a reflection of itself. It sees the people in the world as successful or unsuccessful approximations of its image. Dominance neither respects difference nor values it.

We live in a nation whose increasing diversity makes it hard to keep the illusion of equality while Dominance holds no respect for difference. We can no longer assume the dominance of any cultural viewpoint as the inescapable fact of history, morality, or just sheer numbers.

We can no longer enforce a dominant view as a matter of sheer power. Those who do not share the dominant view are too numerous, refuse to cooperate, and have become too skeptical about the promise of equal status to be content with just a promise.

If the assurance of equality means little unless you see that I am like you, then I shall always be at a disadvantage to you. You and I are not the same.

You likely will be better at being you than will I. Should we then proceed on such a basis to pass out the good and bad things of this world, you will more likely get the good things. Your equality will mean only disparity for me.

II. Equality, Diversity, and the Implications of Dominance

In a society of many cultures, can equality exist without diversity? Your commitment to treat similarly those people who are similarly skilled may fall short if you have trouble assessing the skills of those who are different from you. If you cannot value difference as well as you value the familiar, can you treat equally people who are like you and those who are different?

Dominance, diversity and equality cannot exist together. In a diverse world, equality cannot be without diversity, and neither can exist with Dominance.

III. Understanding Diversity

In many areas of law, diversity serves important governmental interests. With free speech, protecting the diversity of opinions is the cornerstone of constitutional liberty. The economic premise of our antitrust laws is that the economy benefits from diversity in the marketplace and suffers when there is the undue dominance of any one participant.

However, in social relations, diversity remains suspect. We believe that diversity cannot work, and that diversity and competence are mutually exclusive.

A. A Nation Starving for Talent: *The Need for Inclusion*

Our objective is to array the best talent available for the most effective use. Nothing in that statement speaks about equality or diversity. Yet, when we think what the world looks like, these issues inevitably arise. Are we selecting enough talent to meet our present needs? Are we overlooking reserves of talent it might otherwise be useful to tap?

As a nation, we are not identifying enough talent, in quality or in numbers, to meet our developing needs. In the past, we relied upon a demographically limited source of talent: White males. We are changing demographically. The work force of the future will have a greater proportion of females and non-whites.

As the proportion of White males in an expanding work force shrinks, and as the talent available, even in that pool, diminishes, we have more need to tap talent resources we had excluded before. As we meet more competition in the world, the need for expanding the nation's talent reserves becomes even more critical.

B. Expanding the Talent Pool by Tapping New Cultural Reserves: *The Lesson of Baseball*

From the start, the game of baseball was tainted by the same inequality that infested the nation. It excluded talented ball players from the game solely because of skin color. This inequality persisted until April 15, 1947. On that date, Jackie Robinson appeared in the starting lineup for the Brooklyn Dodgers.

Baseball then began an experiment in diversity that continues today. Understanding how that experiment worked and did not work gives insight into what diversity can mean. It also shows how we can lose sight of the goal to include those who are different.

Looking beyond 1947, the admission of Robinson changed the fortunes of the Dodgers. That single act may have made them champions on the field and a national draw off.

In the ten years that followed Robinson's entrance into the major leagues, the Dodgers won five National League pennants, and one world series. During this time, a Dodger was named rookie of the year three times, most valuable player five times, and was awarded top pitching honors the only time such honors were given during this span. All of the Dodgers so credited were African Americans. No other Dodgers won such individual post season honors during this same period.

Baseball's experiment in diversity resulted in several accomplishments. Obviously, the Dodgers tapped a rich pool of talent that had previously been off-limits to major league teams. In addition, the Dodgers tapped new markets. By opening the game to African Americans, the Dodgers won fans from a community that baseball had before shunned.

The baseball experiment in diversity, however, warrants further reflection. It is obvious that the public became blessed to witness remarkable accomplishments by extraordinary athletes. The game itself, however, was not significantly changed.

Baseball removed the bar to major league play for African Americans. However, it may have merely made color a qualification for advancement to other places in its structure.

The lesson of baseball may be how diversity does not work. In assessing the diversity of any system, the test is how deep or how high diversity can be found.

How diverse are those players having marginal, not spectacular, skill? There is always room for a superstar of remarkable physical ability. Marginal players, however, have a job only because someone chooses to appreciate their limited skills and find a place for them. Baseball's limited commitment to diversity may be reflected in the composition of its pool of journeyman players and the absence of comparable diversity there.

CLAIRVOYANCE

The assessment of marginal talent also determines who falls within the leadership pool. If leaders are selected based on certain intangibles, rather than physical abilities alone, leaders are selected on the same basis as marginal players. It is no surprise then that many baseball managers were themselves players of undistinguished achievement. Further, it is no surprise that diversity is found least among the ranks not only of these baseball field leaders, but also among those in baseball's front offices.

The lesson that baseball offers may be less about how to make diversity work than how to exploit new talent pools for limited purposes. Baseball reflects the benefits of such exploitation, without showing much evidence of diversity beyond the field of play.

It has recognized the African American athlete. The African American manager has yet to win comparable distinction. The African American general manager has yet even to appear any time during the 45 years since Jackie Robinson took the field.

More telling is the extent to which the infusion of new talent has affected how the game is played. The economics of the game has changed. The psychology of the players has changed as well. Yet, baseball remains largely unaffected by the inclusion of African Americans.

John McGraw, the field leader of the New York Giants in the early part of this century, could take over his Giants, now in San Francisco, and manage a game without much need for adjustment. Baseball has opened its doors to the African American athlete, but perhaps not its mind and soul.

C. Benefitting from the Operation of Diversity: *The Lesson of Basketball*

Basketball, like baseball, is an American game with roots in our nation's racially segregated past. Like professional baseball, basketball had its color line, and that bar persisted after the elimination of the bar in baseball.

Unlike baseball, it is hard to imagine any basketball coach from the early part of the century coaching the game as it is now played. In addition, African Americans not only are represented generally throughout the ranks of players, including the marginal players. They also have been represented among the coaches, the general managers, and, for a short time, one owner group.

Why is basketball different? It has not made itself a martyr to social justice for diversity at the cost of popularity. A short time ago, in the late 1970s, the concern was that basketball had become "too Black" to survive as a sport of general appeal.

Yet, in a short time, the sport has earned remarkable popularity without turning its back on any constituency. Rather, it has embraced them all.

In contrast, baseball has declining popularity within the African American market that the Dodgers first courted 45 years ago. As a diversity system, basketball has worked differently.

A significant difference between the two sports is game structure. Baseball is conservative. It has almost religious reverence for its unchanging structure.

CLAIRVOYANCE

Basketball is far more free and far less structured in determining outcomes. In the fluidity of its pace and structure, basketball is a game of constantly changing possibility.

Baseball is a game of static positions with well-defined functions and roles. In basketball, any player can defend any other opposing player. Any player can score in any number of ways. In basketball, there is a greater array of winning options for a more varied array of skills. Thus, the structure of basketball better accommodates difference.

An additional factor promoting diversity in basketball has been its openness to talent from different communities. In basketball, the mainstream has not dominated all aspects of the sport and dictated modes of play. Perhaps, more than the elimination of the color line, the acceptance of "the playground", as a nurturer of talent and innovation, has permitted basketball to derive the fullest benefit from diversity.

We play games in many arenas below the professional level. Children played stick ball in the streets of New York City years ago. We played games as students in fields and diamonds adjacent to our schools. There are softball leagues that include grown men and women. Amid the harsh realities of urban poverty, young men and old men pursue dreams of glory on the hard asphalt of inner city basketball courts. Despite this swell of activity below the level of professional scrutiny, not every sandlot emerges as a *playground*.

A *playground* exists apart from the mainstream of play in a particular sport. It defines its own values. It creates its own solutions to the problems of play. It seeks out its own stars. It determines its own success. Most important, it provides its own identity to those who play -- without reference to the mainstream.

For basketball, the *playground* has been an arena of play that has resisted the dominance of the mainstream. Through the *playground*, outsiders can participate in the mainstream, not as mere invitees to be schooled in the ways the game, but as ambassadors from a foreign land possessing valuable goods in their own right. In this way, the game did not succeed in transforming its outsiders within accepted molds, but allowed the outsiders to transform the game.

Within the context of basketball, the *playground* has provided a separate subculture of play that has permitted the game to translate difference into value. The playground game is different from the mainstream game of amateur and professional basketball.

A player from the playground comes with something different to share with the mainstream, not just an athletic body to be trained and molded in the image of mainstream play. Because the value of difference can be shown on the playground, that showing can open not only the eyes of the game, but its mind, as well, to the unknown possibilities offered by other cultures.

Basketball and baseball represent what may be distinctly different solutions to the problem of organizing cultures. Baseball has tried to make a unified culture within which all players must conform. Basketball has accepted the benefits offered by other basketball cultures and created a mainstream that is more a cultural *marketplace* than *melting pot*.

CLAIRVOYANCE

By opening the major leagues to African American players, baseball secured a unified culture at the expense of its playground -- the Negro Leagues. With the demise of the Negro Leagues, baseball deprived itself of a key resource to spark change and cultivate an appreciation of difference.

For baseball, the Negro Leagues were where other solutions to baseball problems had been developed and a new array of baseball skills identified in the hothouse of an outside subculture. Without this subculture, baseball made White ball players and African American ball players indistinguishable.

Excluding differences in individual physical gifts, baseball made all ball players effectively the same. In a culture of inherent inequality, however, making everyone functionally the same does not promote equality. Instead, it entrenches inequality.

In a system of inherent inequality, a choice of candidates having comparable skill, but differing backgrounds, always disfavors the outsider. Paradoxically, breaking the color bar, with destruction of the Negro Leagues, may have doomed African Americans to inequality in baseball.

Basketball diversity has several different features: (1) strong and autonomous game subcultures that develop varied solutions to the common problems of the game; (2) a mainstream marketplace capable of exchanging the varied currencies of these different subcultures into a common economy of winning; and (3) a recognition that the utility of the marketplace is in maintaining the strength of the subcultures outside the mainstream.

Once the mainstream owns or controls the subcultures that nourish it, the mainstream loses the benefit of diversity that the subcultures provide. The single difference between a *melting pot* and a *marketplace* is the presence of dominance as an essential element of one and its necessary absence from the other.

D. The Melting Pot and the Marketplace

We have lived in a world of many cultures since the beginning of civilization. Living with other cultures is not at all new. What is recent is our awareness of the varying ways in which we can organize multicultural life.

It is an implication of Dominance to assume that several cultures can only function with a center of focus that must be *my* culture. Such has been the premise of what has been called here the *melting pot.*

The *melting pot* represents a model for organizing interaction among groups around the standards and assumptions of a dominant group. The best known example of the melting pot model is the experience of American immigration. From the early 19th century to the present generation, we expect that outsiders will learn, and adapt to, the prevailing culture.

Because many of us take the melting pot for granted, we overlook the values inherent in the model. The model values assimilation and discounts difference. It entrenches the standards and values of the dominant culture over those of the outsider. It makes assimilation to the dominant culture a badge of acceptance for outsiders. Consequently, for the outsider, participation within the dominant culture is secured at the price of assimilation.

The outsider may, however, be valuable as outsider. He may see things differently. He may think about things differently. He may do things differently. We can learn a great deal from having to look at ourselves and our world through someone else's eyes.

Do we not lose the insight of his perspective by insisting that the outsider remake himself in our image? Do we not silence him from offering us the solutions apparent from his vantage when the arrogance of our own assumptions makes his difference from us a matter of his shame?

The melting pot is not a model that favors innovation or accommodates difference. It promotes, at least, the *appearance* of fellowship by its acceptance of the outsider prepared to fit inside. However, if the *appearance* of fellowship does not extend to those who fail to fit in, the melting pot may quickly degenerate into a powder keg.

The *marketplace* is a model of multicultural organization based upon the participation of several groups in a common activity, rather than their blending into a common culture. It represents the bazaar of cultural exchange, in which cultural perspectives interact, transact, and otherwise wheel and deal for mutual benefit.

This cultural market, like its economic analogue, is driven by the freedom it gives participants to set value based upon the recognized need to exchange and induce exchange. The driving force of this market is not the interworking of demand and supply. Rather, it is the interweaving of differing perspectives to generate new solutions to create value.

The marketplace organizes cultural activity around problem-solving to achieve a cultural equilibrium. The melting pot, on the other hand, secures cultural stability around the dominance of a single culture as a necessary condition for solving problems.

The two frameworks for cultural organization represent alternate approaches to the fundamental problem of inclusion. In a world of many cultures, does a society hold itself together by finding a solution toward which everyone can contribute or must we first find out how to force people to work together to get anything to work?

When we look at the world around us, we must decide which model works better. Each model carries advantages and weaknesses.

The melting pot places a premium on assimilation. Without the acceptance of assimilation, the melting pot does not work. It just produces more people who fall outside the mainstream, contribute little and take a lot. In time, exclusion destroys the melting pot.

On the other hand, the marketplace requires activity outside the mainstream. If many people are indifferent to what goes on outside the mainstream so as not to deal outside the mainstream, then the marketplace just collapses into chaos.

However, if it is desirable to bring together people that the melting pot cannot assimilate, the marketplace solution may be the only choice. Yet, making that choice work may be harder than just choosing the *marketplace* as a model.

IV.   Equal Protection in the Melting Pot and the Marketplace

In the melting pot, we practice equality by treating people the same once they are within the mainstream. We accept the results of this equality, despite any persistent disparity, just as long as admission to the mainstream remains open to all.

The law of equal protection has been the rule of equal opportunity within the mainstream. It has not looked at the nature of the invitation to the mainstream.

The controlling assumption of Dominance is that if we are all the same, then everyone else must be like me. The melting pot also makes the comparable assumption that we all want to be the same, and that we all want to be like me. Accordingly, the law protects equally by assuring the opportunity of all to be treated like me, as long as they are like me -- or want to be.

The marketplace functions differently. The marketplace promotes equality by the free activity of the market. The cultural market -- not the law of the mainstream -- sets the values and standards that would otherwise be applied to determine who is entitled to comparable treatment or what treatment is comparable.

The currency of the cultural market, as with any market, is utility. In the marketplace, the law protects equally by protecting the market and assuring participation -- not just the *opportunity* to participate -- in the market.

As it has in the commercial market, the law would protect in this cultural market by keeping dominance out. To do that, it must allow the market to seek out the diverse wares necessary to sustain the market's activity. To sustain its activity, the market needs difference to induce the exchange it requires.

A market in the same resource floods this cultural economy and brings to a halt the activity that sustains the market. Such activity is the cultural glue of a marketplace society.

The law of equal protection in the melting pot is deliberately blind to diversity and offers little to promote it. The melting pot requires assimilation and accepts difference only after it has been assimilated to be acceptable within dominant standards.

How can the law of equal protection accommodate diversity? It must first understand an equality that recognizes difference. The law must question the underlying assumption that either we are all the same or want to be. Accordingly, the law must abandon its melting pot assumptions and embrace the marketplace.

To embrace the marketplace, the law must accept the assumptions of the marketplace. It must reject, for example, the "one way" solution.

In the marketplace, there is never just one way to do anything. There is no one set of skills to achieve a given task, but an array of varied skills and approaches. With an array of skills and approaches, the marketplace is open to a variety of otherwise suitable candidates, with no special deference to any one.

The marketplace discounts the notion of relative qualification. The idea that someone might be more qualified than someone else to do a task has no meaning. The candidate either can or cannot do the job. The job he does is not more or less done depending upon the extent of his qualifications.

In the marketplace, difference exists without hierarchy. Any one solution takes care of a problem no less and no more than any other.

The cultural market functions freely and establishes its own equilibrium. In the marketplace, the law does not enforce a particular rule of equality. The free activity of the market affords equality to all who participate.

As long as the market remains open to all, and as long as all can participate without the dominance of any particular viewpoint, the market establishes its own standards far better than any court of law. Under the rule of the marketplace, the law works best just by letting the market function free of Dominance.

Finally, a marketplace cannot exist outside Dominance without playgrounds. The marketplace requires these special places outside the mainstream to give difference value. Playgrounds are essential to establishing both equality and diversity.

Playgrounds empower people *outside the mainstream*. Such empowered people deal with the mainstream from the standpoint of the differences that set them apart.

These differences also define the outsider by what uniquely he can offer. These differences, by virtue of his uniqueness, give him a value that has nothing to do with how closely he might approximate the mainstream and ignore who he is. These differences, therefore, empower the outsider to be who he is -- an outsider. That kind of empowerment is the only *equality* that can exist in a multicultural world.

We invoke equality to compare what you can do that I cannot, or *vice versa*. If I am empowered to do what I choose to do, what you can do matters not at all to me. Such is the only equality meaningful to both you and me in our difference. Such equality requires no comparison of me with you or you with me that can only create an inequality that belies all the professions of good will about our common humanity.

Once *equality* is meaningful as my empowerment simply to be whoever I choose -- without reference to you -- it also becomes superfluous. I am no longer controlled by the invidious comparisons to you implied in any consideration of *our* equality.

Our equality then can only be inherently *unequal*. I am thus *your* equal, only as long as I compare favorably to you. How then can *our* equality be equal when it depends upon you as the standard of *our* comparability?

Only *my* equality can be meaningfully equal and, at the same time, utter nonsense. Once these implied comparisons with you have no significance in deciding what is equal, can *equality* serve any purpose at all for us? Yet, is this not the only time we can be said to be truly comparable in our necessary and mutual disregard of one another?

The ultimate paradox of equality then is that we have not achieved it until we have made our craving for it obsolete. To do that, we must learn how to function outside the dominance of anyone else.

CLAIRVOYANCE

To function in this way is to empower ourselves. To confront the arrogance of Dominance, we must dare live without the familiarity of its limiting assumptions and within the understanding of our own *autonomy* that Dominance has denied of ourselves and of others.

CLAIRVOYANCE

Them that's got shall get.
Them that's not shall lose.
So the Bible says.
And it still is news.
Mama may have.
Papa may have.
But God bless the child that's got his own.

Billie Holiday,
God Bless the Child

Seeing Clearly Housing Options

Initial Thoughts about Housing

This effort begins with the unremarkable realization that the interests of African Americans in housing for African Americans need not be the same as the interests of other people in housing for African Americans. We are not just looking for affordable shelter. When the policy is done, and the housing is built, we don't get to go home somewhere else. We have to live, work, and raise our children with the decision.

We are not just looking to help someone else. We are looking to make for ourselves something we would want for ourselves. From this standpoint, the question of housing does not end -- or even begin -- with building houses. It rests in building communities: places not just where people live, but where they can grow and prosper.

For us, community arises from the foundation of *choice* and *autonomy*. Community cannot arise unless we can be said to *choose* to live with the people who are our neighbors. Otherwise, we are no more than inmates in the prison of our circumstance. Choice has no meaning without autonomy: the power freely to set for myself what I would choose for myself.

You might ask why *community* for African Americans rests upon the cornerstones of choice and autonomy. There was a time not that long ago when African Americans joined in community without much that passed either for choice or autonomy. Not just the law, but everyone's expectations, laid out clear boundaries where African Americans could and could not live, whatever their economic circumstance.

Yet, look closer. Little of what the people then accomplished, or tried to accomplish, could have been done without the desire, at least, to choose a better life. In our communities today, the prospect of a better life is seen as so remote that we have become the prisoners of our own limiting expectations for ourselves.

In such a limiting world, we deny ourselves the *chance* for either *choice* or *autonomy*. It matters little how close the reality of it might be to us.

On the other hand, paying the price of greater affluence in a culture not our own, we deny ourselves the reality of choice by grasping at its illusion. The option to live someone else's dream offers me no choice at all. I can only *choose* when I am free not just to do as I choose, but to choose as I would -- to set for myself a full array of possible outcomes.

For autonomy to be real, I have to be able to do something about what I would otherwise choose. To have such autonomy, I require economic independence. While I do not have to choose to live like you, I still have to be able to live as I choose for me.

In the real world, such choice requires income, savings, investment, business, markets, and economic security. We therefore cannot think of housing without also thinking economics.

If I have *choice* and *autonomy*, certain things become unimportant. Perhaps the least important of these concerns is the fact that some would-be neighbors would choose not to live with me.

As African Americans, our focus is on African Americans. That there may be people of European descent who choose not to be our neighbors and leave the place we would choose to live is of no great concern. The community we must build does not immediately involve them nor immediately require them. It does, however, require the best of us.

In this sense, as we look at the demographics of our community, we must understand the value we represent in our difference. We represent a varied range of perspectives from the most remote board room to the bleakest back alley. There is much we have seen as a community and much any one of us alone will never see. We need a community of vision to see our own progress.

Our communities therefore require demographics expansive enough to include all of us. To hold it together, we need a strong and independent middle class core around which we can transform, generate, and sustain values that work for us to live together in our own prosperity.

As we begin to refashion our own categories of thinking about our own communities, we start with the following precepts:

- Choice is the fundamental element of our housing policy.
- Home ownership is its principal goal.
- The market is not evil. It is just not ours. Too long, we have been captive to our own fear of markets to shy away from transforming an economy to work for us.
- Economic integration, transcending the class distinctions among ourselves, is the only basis for African American

community -- and the only real hope for American community.

- A solution for the woes of poor Black folk is creating rich Black folk -- the belief in our own wealth as a solution to our own poverty.
- White flight is not a relevant concern of ours. Black flight is.
- Perceptions lie at the heart of the problem of changing the housing patterns in our cities. The problem is greatest among other African Americans.
- We do not have to save every Black person in America. We need only create a community in which it is realistic to expect that all African Americans can prosper.
- We cannot assume that everyone in our community wants what we want. We can only provide the opportunity and autonomy for each to choose as each would. The only thing we all want is choice and the autonomy to choose as we would.
- We have to offer different kinds of housing products to meet the varied needs of a varied community. Not everyone wants the same thing.
- The aim of low income housing is to create high income housing: to make itself -- and the poverty it entrenches -- obsolete.

Sylvia's Choice:
A Story of a Future Rich in Options

by
John H. Morris, Jr.

> *Sylvia awoke from a fitful sleep still undecided. She had gone to bed the night before convinced that her ship had come in.*
>
> *She had before her an offer to buy the home she had grown up in for more money than she had ever seen in her life. Yet, after tossing and turning, and getting up and lying back down, and rubbing her temples raw for an answer that never seemed to materialize, Sylvia was tired, scared, and not a little bit punch drunk.*
>
> *Still, she had to go to work. She shaded her eyes, as the morning sun filtered through the back window of her bedroom. Its light reflected off the computer screen at the foot of her bed where last night Sylvia had spent so much time reviewing and reviewing again the numbers from Dr. Boyd's offer.*
>
> *She was expected to process more data she barely understood on the research project her team at the University was near completing. Yet today, she just wanted to call in sick, if only to get some rest, if not more time to ponder her future.*

CLAIRVOYANCE

Sylvia forced herself to turn on the radio. The morning newscast brought her out of her own sleepless lethargy back to the reality of the present.

It was June 5, 2015. She was an information specialist assigned to the oncological research group of the University of Maryland School of Medicine. She was a 27-year-old single mother, trying to complete the requirements for a college degree. She lived with her mother in the Lexington Terrace village, Du Bois Circle. They had lived in the same home since 1997, when they first leased the then newly-built townhouse as public housing tenants. Like their neighbors, they were buying their unit from the City.

Now, she faced the specter of gentrification. Sylvia had before her an offer from a rising African American doctor teaching at the Medical School to buy her home for $130,000. She and her mother would clear from this sale -- if they went forward with it -- nearly $100,000. She had had the offer for about two weeks, and, today, the doctor, Larry Boyd, wanted an answer. Sylvia somehow was still undecided.

Sylvia put aside the problems of the moment and set about starting her day. She stumbled from her room to the bedroom her daughter, Sara, shared with the little girl's grandmother. As she left her room, Sylvia heard her mother, Pat, moving about downstairs. She moved a little more briskly into Sara's room and stirred the 8-year-old into consciousness again.

The school year was ending. Sara would walk to Lexington Terrace Elementary School with her grandmother. Pat worked at the Village's Children Center, located at the elementary school. There, Pat and the other Center elders looked after the Village children before and after the school day, into the evening hours while parents worked. Her pay from the Center, combined with Sylvia's income from the Medical School, had qualified both Sylvia and Pat for the unit buy-back program.

Sylvia quickly scanned the homework that Sara had left. In her worry of the night before, she could focus on little else. This morning, she could barely direct enough attention to notice much more than that Sara had correctly spelled her name and had filled out a page of math problems. Sylvia prayed that the work had been done right and quickly placed the paper among Sara's school things.

As Sara yawned and stretched, Sylvia softly said, "You have a clean uniform in the closet, baby." With a bit more firmness, she added, "Make sure you wear that one," placing her hand on the recently ironed uniform skirt.

Sylvia spent some time with her mother on the matter of their choice. She had spent time with her mother the night before, and, still, they were undecided.

To her great disappointment, Pat was not much help. After listening to Sylvia walk through the options after a night's sleeplessness, Pat could only sigh, "Just trust in the Lord, Honey. Whatever you decide will be all right by Him, and that'll be all right by me."

Sylvia tried not to roll her eyes, or at least not to let her mother notice her mounting exasperation. She had to make some choice, and she was still undecided.

Pat and Sara left for school. Sylvia was alone in her home. Perhaps, she pondered, it would be the last time that she would really be alone in her home. She had about an hour before she would be late for work.

She thought about going back up to her room to her computer to run the numbers again. She had done that last night, and still she was undecided.

She just sat on the living room sofa she and her mother had been so fond of when they first saw it down-town. She stretched out a bit, and just thought, and thought, and thought and . . . .

It seemed so easy last night after dinner. Then, she didn't have a moment's hesitation. Here she was, with an offer to clear $100,000 to leave a place her mother would have killed to leave 20 years before. She had the money to go to a neighborhood her mother would have died for.

So why then was she so undecided now? Was it sentiment? Was it just a lack of confidence that she could make the right decision?

She had barely finished high school and was strug-gling to get through college. She might never see so much money at one time again, short of winning the *lottery that she and her mother so often played and as often lost.*

But, Sylvia pondered still. Here was this doctor, a man she had come both to like and respect. He was willing to pay $130,000 just to own her house. He probably would pay a lot more to fashion the house to his taste and that of his family. He was no fool. Why didn't he want to run away, as so many of her friends from childhood had years ago?

Sylvia startled a bit. She was on to something. This was a new thought. She followed its course. Dr. Boyd was a doctor. He made a lot more money than she did. Still, he was a Black man in a world not particularly friendly to Black people.

He could not have $130,000 and more laying around at his disposal. She was sure that he had the $130,000 he had offered to her. She wondered now where he got it.

She had not thought about that before. At that moment, it occurred to her that, like everybody else she knew of who had bought a home, Dr. Boyd had to have gone to a bank for the money he was going to pay her.

Now, not only did she have Dr. Boyd investing in her house, she had a bank with him. She thought some more. She wasn't aware of any special government programs that Dr. Boyd might be eligible for to assist him in getting this loan. If Dr. Boyd had a loan from a bank to buy her house, he had to have gone to a real bank, one of those downtown banks she used to think would never even give people like her the time of day.

She kept thinking. She liked this course she was following. What did Dr. Boyd want her house for? Of course, it was convenient. She knew that. In less than an hour, she would be leaving her door to walk to work.

It then occurred to her that she had no car. She had not thought about it before, but she had functioned in DuBois Circle without a car. The doctors for her daughter and her mother were the same walk away as work. There were doctors even closer in the Village.

The city villages had their own markets, a mixture of the suburban old supermarket chains and nearby Lexington Market. Downtown was just a subway ride away. Without a car, she effortlessly could go to the Inner Harbor and the other downtown amenities.

Still, she found much of her life focused in DuBois Circle. She bought her food there. She bought her clothes there. She even had bought her computer there and had it serviced at another shop in the Village. Her bank was in the Village.

She looked around her townhouse. What was so special about this place that someone would offer $130,000, as is? It had not been painted for a while. It was simply arranged. She had found the space, however, ample not only for her needs, but those of her mother.

Sylvia's bedroom was huge. So was that where her mother and daughter slept. Sylvia had had few problems with the unit since she and her mother first occupied it in 1997, just after it had been built.

Once, she recalled the toilets getting backed up and remembered the plumber remarking how easy it was to get at the pipes. He even offered a deal to put in a bathroom off her bedroom, noting that the addition would be such a snap.

Sylvia looked around with new eyes. The early morning sunlight made the room alive with a brightness that dressed up even the old discount furniture Sylvia and her mother could afford. With some paint, she thought, some new additions, and the money she knew that Dr. Boyd could get beyond the $130,000, the house could be made to be just wonderful.

She remembered, as a girl, hearing some people talk about the old 'Dollar Houses' the White folks long before remade into great homes, until they sold out to leave the City. The thought teased her that she could do that but stay where she grew up.

Then reality began to tug at her soaring feet. "It's one thing," Sylvia noted, "for Dr. Boyd to do all these things with the house. Why, he's a doctor with money, a high paying job, and people who will vouch for him. It's another thing for me to do this. Where do I get the money?"

CLAIRVOYANCE

That thought weighed her down. It seemed that a cloud had come out and shaded the luster of the morning she had earlier warmed in. As the light retreated and the room darkened, so too did Sylvia's vision. It was a nice dream, but it wouldn't work. She was soberly awake now.

She stirred from the sofa and heavily lifted herself up the stairs, into her second floor hallway, and into the bathroom. She prepared to go to work, still undecided.

Time passed. Sylvia quickened her pace, as she made the final preparations to transform herself into the stunning creature she wanted everyone at work to see.

She raced down the steps, checking her watch, knowing how much time she needed for the walk across the Village to the Medical School. Then she stopped dead in her tracks as she opened her door.

The thought hit her. It startled her, and it shook her out of her gloom. "You know," she said to herself. "I'd rather have Dr. Boyd as a neighbor than as a buyer. He has the money. He wants to buy into the Village. Someone will sell to him. It doesn't have to be me.

"If I stay, my house is worth more to me with him next door than with him here and me buying somewhere else. I got to find a way to make staying work. I just can't stay an Information Specialist at the Medical School much longer. But what else? What can I do for the money to make my house the place I saw this morning?"

Sylvia then went to work, still undecided -- not about what to tell Dr. Boyd, but about what she was going to do about it after she told him.

As we consider the array of desirable options for people in our community to confront their housing choices, we have in mind the story of Sylvia, her wealth of possible options, and her ability to see them.

Housing Issues:
Building New Community

What is the objective that our thinking on housing should achieve? It is not necessarily a place I could comfortably wish other people could live in.

As an African American, the point of any policy for African Americans must be to create a community I want for myself. No matter who may live in such a community, if it is occupied largely by African Americans, it is inevitably *my* community.

I may live somewhere else. Still, the shaping of my identity, the security of my livelihood, and the focus of my economic well-being depend on how well people like me manage to get along.

In this regard, notions of community have substance and meaning beyond the platitudes of collaborative living we often hear or the points we may find on a map. Community is that place any people must have to grow independent and strong. It is that place they look to not just to define who they are but to

61

show what it is about themselves that gives them inherent value --
to themselves and to anyone else.

Such a place must provide the prospect and the substance of
prosperity, not just for the people who live there, but for everyone
else who may depend upon the people who live there. Such
community begins with housing. It ends with realizing the dreams
and aspirations of a people.

The issues of housing for such *community* go far beyond
providing cheap and available dwellings. In looking at building
such community, we start by rethinking the basic assumptions
that have informed our thinking on housing. We have thus
focused on four areas: (1) community design; (2) the economics
of community; (3) the values of community; and (4) the demographics of community.

The issue of design proceeds from the naive question of what
such a community of African Americans must look like to achieve
the purposes of African Americans, given the present circumstances of African Americans. The issues of economics raise
those questions of what such community must do to support
financially its own dreams. The community must also nurture its
own way of thinking. How the community views itself, the world,
and the things its people need to do involves the question of
values. Finally, who must make up this community to nurture the
values and create the economy is key to the issue of demographics.

1. ***Community Design:*** The Village, as the autonomous, self contained housing cluster or neighborhood, forms the basic unit of organization. It is comprised of
   - Mixed income families
   - Homes designed to be improved, not disposed of
   - Economies developed to make ownership more than less possible
   - A business base in which residents have an ownership stake
   - Systems in place controlled by the residents to do all of the above things.

Related issues:

- Creating construction techniques to build quality houses more cheaply for improvement and expansion, not disposal. For example, design must address how to devise electrical, plumbing or heating systems so that home additions can be more cheaply done without having to redo these basic home systems
- Developing a supporting home improvement industry, instead of promoting real estate sales agencies
- Tying design considerations to infrastructure needs for business development, entrepreneurial development (micro-business support), communications, education, health care, transportation, retail amenities, child and adolescent care, and public safety
- Easing the permit approval process for cheap home improvement
- Creating entities for more decentralized governance of community activities

- Creating entities in which residents can financially participate in the economic development of the community
- Resolving housing density issues

2. *Community Economics:* Using government housing policy as an economic engine to make residents in our community participants in their own economy. To create such favorable economic conditions, we must

- Have mixed income housing
- Have an economy that creates enough jobs and other opportunities to add value to support the aspirations and dreams of the people in the community
- Envision economic development projects to provide the setting for economic independence, *e.g.*, a shopping center with community economic participation, a small business incubator, or business office support center providing, for a number of ventures, office services with word processing, mail access, fax capability, accounting and legal services, and a community health care delivery system
- Create a burgeoning craftsman class to serve the housing and business maintenance and equipment needs for our community to grow
- Develop a community economic infrastructure, *i.e.*, systems to make it easier for people within the community to do more business with one another than with those outside the community, and systems to allow the community to transact most effectively with outside commercial interests

- Provide financing: Over 50% from African American controlled sources, such as
  - ▸ Black religious institutions
  - ▸ Local housing authority: use of influence to find financial partners and use of Block Grant funds
  - ▸ Reliance upon such other community institutions, particularly historically black institutions, such as Coppin State College and Morgan State University in Baltimore, to add economic value
  - ▸ Capital from anticipated development of community economy to keep dollars in the community and to exploit future economic opportunities in technology and other industry sectors
- Promote public safety
- Creatively use community assets
- Focus on building high income, not just low income, housing
- Provide participation by middle class people.

Related issues:

- Identifying and cataloguing community assets
- Developing a system to quantify, express, and predict economic growth in African American communities
- Creating entities owned by African Americans to exploit economic opportunities in African American communities, to be owned by African Americans and to provide profits to African Americans and the residents of the community

- Designing structures to translate productive community behavior into personal economic benefit
- Creating a financing vehicle for African American communities to raise capital
- Identifying suitable people of talent to run and operate economic entities successfully in African American communities
- Projecting future economic opportunities to engage African Americans in future profits

3. *The Values of Community*: To create the climate in which people can be mutually supportive of one another, we need to

- Enhance the presence of a middle class
- Emphasize and reinforce the institutions that develop and nurture values, such as religious congregations and schools, locally owned businesses, and social organizations
- Link middle class income to communities with fewer resources to provide new value models and promote stability to forge stronger community ties among all of our people.

Related issues:

- Identifying both traditional and new institutions as focuses for values support
- Ascertaining a new role for the family, as nurturer of values, when families may vary in structure and composition
- Clarifying the role of the "village," as shaper of values for all families

- Overcoming the class divisions within our own community to forge a productive relationship between middle class, working class and poor folk
- Creating new myths to support the values we need

4. *The Demographics of Community*: To create the environment conducive of community development, we need a mix of people

- that establishes a "critical mass" of middle class people to fire a more favorable view of future possibilities
- that focuses on home ownership
- that markets the community as a place for people looking to "move up" economically
- that focuses on first time home owners

To achieve such a demographic mix, we have to

- Reduce the concentration of poverty in the community
- Stabilize communities and local public schools
- Provide for public safety
- Locate economic opportunity in the community and use it as a beacon to attract people of talent and initiative

Related issues:

- Addressing the concentration of poor people in our urban centers
- Resolving concerns that White folks may leave -- Do we care?
- Recruiting African Americans from outside the community

Conclusion

Current housing policy is based upon assumptions and premises that African Americans cannot accept. African Americans cannot accept the premise that it is enough just to house those who cannot afford shelter when the result is housing that keeps African Americans in poverty.

The goal of housing ought not just be getting people off the street, but keeping people on their feet, moving toward their own independence. In the long run, having *your own roof* over your head may be more important than just keeping out the rain.

With different assumptions, African Americans can transform, *for ourselves,* the urban centers in which we now live into places that we, and anyone else, would want to live.

The souls of Black folk require a good degree of attention, particularly now. Otherwise, the community we create for a contented, but soulless, population will inevitably fail to sustain itself. Soulless people value little, let alone themselves and their own future.

Ultimately, all of us have to recognize that we cannot build community just with brick and mortar. Community arises only from body and soul.

For community to arise from brick and mortar, the people who occupy the brick and mortar must have *choice* and *autonomy*. It is through the choices we make that we are who we are. Without the ability to choose for ourselves, we become a people without an identity -- a people without a soul. People without a soul can form nothing that works as *community*.

We can provide palatial settings for people to live. Yet, unless that setting also affords them choice and autonomy, it is just a lavish and very accommodating prison.

The point then of a housing policy that works for African Americans is to create real options for African Americans to be whoever we choose to be. The point of such housing is not just to shelter people, but to provide the setting for a productive life.

As we make policy in housing for African Americans, as African Americans, we make policy for housing not the tired bodies of the poor, but the souls of rising people. Only African Americans can make that policy from which true community can arise. It is in the very making of policy that we affirm who we are -- and affirm the community that would emerge from our choices.

More directly, we have to understand that notion of community and how the techniques for building *communities* -- not houses -- will differ accordingly to reflect the body and soul of its members. These requirements of body and soul will also dictate the qualifications and requirements of whoever will be the builder of this new community. More than not, the builder must be from the community to emerge. We then can be the only builders of our own community.

CLAIRVOYANCE

I worked on jobs
With my feet and my hands.
And all the work I did
Was for the other man.
Now we demands a chance
To do things for ourselves.
We're tired of beatin' our heads against the wall
And workin' for someone else.

Say It Loud (I'm Black and I'm Proud)
(James Brown/Alfred Ellis)

The Wealth of Black Folk

Introduction:
We Are the Wealth of Our Community

The wealth of Black folk simply embraces the full value of what we make, what we think, what we do, and what we otherwise have to offer one another and the rest of the world. Often, that value is known and appreciated only by African Americans.

We must manage that value to make it known both to us and the rest of the world. Otherwise, we give it away to anyone bold enough to assert that value for himself, not us, and to demand full payment for himself, not us.

That wealth generally has not been material or conventional. It has not included great natural resources or expanses of developed real estate. It is not represented by a supply of manufactured goods, farm crops or other commodities.

We are the wealth of Black folk. That wealth comprises our labor, our intelligence, our risk taking, our foresight, and our sacrifice. This wealth of ours is largely undervalued by people unlike us who are blind to its realization because they cannot see our worth.

We can lose this wealth altogether, unless we manage to make its value apparent to everyone. If we do not set its price and demand its value, we only cheat ourselves. That value ultimately is our value.

At its most fundamental level, this wealth is personal. It provides the opportunity for us to do the things we would choose to do and still feed our families. It sustains the work that demands our pride. It offers the rewards that allow us to build the future we would choose for ourselves. It gives us a foundation of achievement to nurture in our children the values to move beyond what we have done. It promotes our independence to think as we would, beholden to no one.

In short, this wealth of ours can buy our emancipation. It can make it possible for a people who have owned little in America -- not even themselves -- to belong to themselves in every important respect.

We often see the economy only as dollars and cents, prices and goods, jobs and professions, and capital and investments. These things are clearly part of any economy.

Yet, for African Americans, economy must be about more. The dollars of any economy involving African Americans at any level of management in America are only as valuable as America perceives its Black folk -- and as Black folk perceive themselves.

This economy African Americans would develop is more than the sum of our dollars. It must encompass our value.

To give our dollars the added power of our value, our economy must be grounded in us. It must demonstrate concretely for anyone too blind to see, but not too dumb to count, that what we do is valuable and why it should be valuable to anyone. We must be our principal resource.

The focus of economic development then is to extract for African Americans the wealth of Black folk. Its point is to make it possible for African Americans to secure for ourselves the value we see in whatever we choose to do. It is to allow us to own, in every sense, who we are.

Thoughts About African American Economic Development: *Finding the Community of Interest*

We African Americans are a varied people. While others may view us and see only the least of our community, we see all of our flowering.

We see the college educated. We see the hard working. We see the lofty dreamers. We see the hard bargainers.

We also see those people who have given up hope and stopped trying. We cannot be blind to those of us who go about destroying the fabric of our community.

Yet, only we, as well, see the promise in *all* of us. We cannot miss seeing the promise that others may miss, as these others have also missed seeing the promise in each of us that we alone see.

However we approach economic development, we owe it to ourselves not only to develop the best of us to the fullest, but to provide for realizing, as well, the promise of the least of us. Only in this way do we provide anything of lasting value to any of us. Only in this way will the wealth we create for ourselves continue to grow.

To make it possible for other African Americans to realize their value, we must provide a foundation that secures the value of anything we have, would produce, create or develop. Whatever secures value in the least of us also secures the value of us all.

Without that value, everything we might otherwise achieve is suspect. What we have is valuable then only if others, not like us, recognize its worth and our worth as well.

We speak of economic development and mean many things. We talk about turning dollars around in our community. We debate building businesses owned by African Americans. For a long time, we have focused on jobs. Recently, we have begun to consider wealth.

The idea of economic development is big enough to encompass all these things for African Americans. For us, the focus of economic development is to

- Create wealth for us
- Create a business base integrated both vertically and horizontally in our own community
- Find new economic models that work for us
- Seize value both inside and outside our community
- Find new markets for the products of our effort
- Assume risk for our gain
- Produce goods and services by our community for our community
- Develop capital
- Promote investment
- See the benefits of economics for all members of our community
- Create networks of business ties with one another
- Control how we see the value of what we do

- Provide the things we need for economic growth, including access to capital, trained labor, and a commitment to excellence
- Produce quality goods and services
- Create a way in which African Americans can do better by doing well.

Economic development in the African American community raises questions of wealth and class. Is it enough for the economy to produce wealth for a few? The existence of a class of great wealth does not raise the same questions in other communities. Yet, for African Americans, wealth in America can be racial betrayal, at worst, or callous selfishness, at best.

On the other hand, universal poverty serves no one. Some Black folk may find comfort in shared misery and only a threat in someone else's prosperity. However, the question we may fairly ask is why the wealth of any individual African American should mean anything more to us than the wealth of any other person.

Wealthy people are numerous in America. Most of these people happen not to be African American. There have been wealthy people a long time in America, and the economic lot of Black folk has largely been unaffected.

The question we all must answer is why those African Americans who may never become wealthy themselves need do anything to help other African Americans attain great wealth. The fundamental question posed by African American economic development is how African American wealth necessarily benefits African Americans who are not wealthy.

CLAIRVOYANCE

We must also consider how African Americans who may labor without great wealth can help support and protect the great wealth of a few. The wealth a few of us acquire may be deceptive, if the rest of us are not economically secure.

In accumulating wealth without the rest of us, what do African Americans secure? In America, such wealth may be nothing more than an invitation to a feast at which you may be the meal. How does an economically vital African American community provide the foundation necessary to secure African American wealth?

In approaching economic development as African Americans, we must view the economy we develop as tapping the value of the *whole* community. Without the whole community, the wealth of Black folk may not be ours at all. It may reflect only the willingness of others to accord it value, as it may benefit them -- *not us.* As it may benefit them, others may change their mind about what it is worth to them. In that way, we give to others the power to dictate our worth.

By the same token, none of us is secure without the few of us who may acquire great wealth unashamedly being African American. Otherwise, who invests in the dreams of those who can gain no audience outside our community? Who buys the labor of those whose value has eluded those people outside our community? Who recognizes the opportunity that only people like us see to our benefit? And who has the capital to do something to secure that benefit for people like us?

In this way, we Africans in America share a community of interests that is fundamentally economic. It is our challenge then to convey that economic vision in creating this economy that works for Black folk. This economic community of interests reflects the following ideas:

- In an economy that values Black folk, African American wealth necessarily benefits *all* Black folk.
- The value of African American wealth is the strength of the African American economy supported by the dollars, labor, insights, risk taking, and ideas of all other African Americans.
- To create an African American economy, African Americans must change what we value
  - ► to value who we are, what we think, what we have and what we do
  - ► to value what makes us better, enhances our skills, and improves the product of our efforts
  - ► to value what is the best about us -- not just what we can get by with.
- By working together, we can control conditions and not let conditions control us.
- Ownership offers the ultimate control over the profits and the jobs that business may provide African Americans.
- Ownership requires capital and investment from African American investors and financial institutions, such as banks, savings and loans, credit unions, and investment firms.
- African American business requires support in a loyal customer base of African Americans.
- A loyal customer base of African Americans requires a labor pool of African Americans superbly trained and committed to excellence.

These ideas point toward a future for African Americans that has to be very different from the present or the past. That future commits African Americans to education as an economic issue. It commits African Americans to address questions of public safety as an economic issue. It commits African Americans to transform our relationships with other communities as an economic issue. Most importantly, it commits African Americans to transform our relationships with one another as an economic issue.

The most daunting challenge we face, however, may be us. We have to cast for ourselves a new future that reflects a new economic reality for African Americans. To transcend old differences, overcome old fears, and elevate old expectations, we have to see the future this economy promises as more than worth the effort it may require of us now.

The Takeover:
A Fable about Creating Value

by
John H. Morris, Jr.

She still didn't know what she would tell him about his offer to buy her house. Sylvia knew she could not sell. She just didn't know how she could explain that she was prepared to turn down more money than she had ever dreamed could be written on a check with her name on it.

Dr. Boyd approached. The moment seemed endless. She forced her eyes to the dimly lit screen of her computer terminal, pretending to be totally absorbed in the triviality of her work.

"Well, Sylvia," Dr. Boyd called out to her. "How's the offer? Good enough to get you to accept my money?"

"Huh?" Sylvia feigned surprise by Dr. Boyd's appearance. "I didn't expect to see you today. How are you, Doctor?"

Sylvia swallowed hard when she saw Dr. Boyd look her way and start walking to her work station at the Medical School. "Well," Dr. Boyd offered. "I'm in need of an answer. Do we have a sale or not?"

"I don't think so, Doctor," Sylvia softly uttered, pointedly looking at her computer terminal as she spoke each word.

Sylvia peered blankly at her computer screen, hoping desperately for the moment to end. She waited and said nothing. She heard nothing from Dr. Boyd. She was almost afraid to look up to see if he was still there. She still felt his presence. But, she could not figure out his silence.

Finally, she could stand the suspense no longer. She looked up at the doctor to find him pouring through a ream of papers she couldn't recognize. He seemed totally absorbed in the figures on a spreadsheet, as if he were adding up the numbers in his head. She didn't get it.

CLAIRVOYANCE

One moment the most important thing to the doctor seemed to be whether she would sell him her home on Du Bois Circle. The next moment, something else just seemed to take him to another planet.

"Doc!?" Sylvia called. After she caught his distant gaze, she implored, "What's goin' on?"

"I can't give you any more money, Sylvia," Dr. Boyd said, still distracted by the papers in front of him.

"It's O.K., Doc. I don't want the money to sell the house. I want to keep the house. Maybe, I can find you another buyer on Du Bois -- with all that money you're offering. Maybe, you can help me find some money to fix up my place the way you were going to? Huh? Doc? You think so?"

Dr. Boyd was off navigating the galaxy again. This time, Sylvia had said what she had been afraid to say. She was fearless now. She tugged gently on the doctor's sleeve.

"What about it, Doc?" she asked looking up at him.

Dr. Boyd looked down at Sylvia, still distracted. Then, he looked away. After a few moments, he just said "Maybe. Let's talk at your next break."

Sylvia and Dr. Boyd were oblivious to the world at the far away Hospital cafeteria table. All sorts of papers were on the table in front of the doctor.

"Look, Sylvia," Dr. Boyd explained calmly, "I'd been looking to buy one of the homes on Du Bois Circle a long time. I'm still interested in buying there, both to live in the neighborhood and as an investment. But, right now, I need cash. I thought I had enough to swing your deal, but when you told me that you weren't looking to sell, another thought occurred to me. Would you be interested in lending me money?"

Sylvia was not prepared for this conversation. She did not know how to answer that question. She had about $17 and change in her purse. Somehow, she knew the doctor was not looking for an extra five bucks.

"How much money do you need, Doc?" she asked, more out of curiosity than anything else.

"How 'bout One Hundred Thousand?"

After Sylvia closed her mouth, she reminded Dr. Boyd that, at last count, she had about $600 in savings. "Where am I going to get $100,000 to give you when I don't have it for myself?"

"Sylvia, you have your house. If I could have borrowed the money to buy it, maybe I could arrange for you to borrow the money for my venture."

"Doc, what's this venture?" Sylvia was slowly becoming intrigued.

"Sylvia, we have to talk away from here."

Later that evening, Dr. Boyd and his lawyer met with Sylvia at Du Bois Circle. Seated in her living room, with her mother making coffee in the next room, Sylvia listened intently to lawyer, Patrick Culver, a senior associate at a large downtown law firm.

Culver explained that Dr. Boyd was one of a group of African American doctors who were planning to buy the Lexington Village clinic from the Hospital. With the help of financing secured by a local African American financial firm, the doctors were putting up their own capital of $1,000,000, leveraging another $5,000,000 in financing.

The clinic had become a cash cow for the Hospital. It had provided a steady stream of patients requiring minimal care for subsidized payments that kept the Hospital flush in other respects. The Hospital would not voluntarily part with the clinic -- even for an offer far more generous than any the doctors could manage.

Culver outlined that part of the strategy was for the largely African American medical staff to defect. It was the plan for the doctors to leave the Hospital and take with them as many staff as they could. By disrupting the continued operation of the clinic, they sought to induce the Hospital to accept a cash offer less than it otherwise would find suitable.

Sylvia was interested. She asked what she was required to do. Culver explained that he would arrange for her to secure a loan from the financial people behind the deal, putting up her home as collateral with the financiers.

Thinking along with the lawyer, she pondered how she would repay the loan. Culver responded that once the deal went through, as a creditor of the venture, she would be repaid from the clinic profits, and she could then repay her loan.

Sylvia asked, "What happens if this doesn't work?"

"Well," Culver's voice lowered, "You probably lose your home. If the foreclosure sale does not clear enough to repay the loan, then you'll owe the finance people the rest. Probably, you declare bankruptcy. However, if we are right -- and we are right -- and the clinic continues to be run as it has been, the profits it creates will take care of your debt and you'll earn interest."

Sylvia knew about loans. "I don't have income to handle the monthly payments on $100,000, even with help from the clinic."

Culver offered, "Sylvia, if we structured a deal you could live with, could we use your collateral for our venture?"

Sylvia thought a bit. She asked, "What do I get for my trouble here?"

Culver tried to explain that Sylvia would get a modest return on the loan, between one and two percentage points on the $100,000, after all interest was taken care of.

Sylvia quickly calculated. "Just $2,000 a year. Just for the privilege of maybe losing my house. I don't know?"

Culver and Dr. Boyd left with no commitment from Sylvia. After they left, Sylvia talked with her mother.

CLAIRVOYANCE

"What do you think I should do, Mama?"

"Why are you asking me? I don't know nothing about no high finance. All I know is that if you gonna gamble with money you can't afford to lose, you better make sure you don't and make damn sure you get enough money to make the gamble worth the risk."

Sylvia thought about her mother's advice. She then asked her mother about all the old ladies she worked with at the Village's Children Center. They laughed about all the sons and daughters and grandchildren these old ladies had who still lived in Lexington Village. It seemed to Sylvia that just about everybody in Lexington Village knew her mother or her mother knew them.

With little fanfare, the Black doctors at the medical center left the clinic. Their standing offer of $6,000,000 for the clinic the Hospital rejected out of hand. Victor Freeland, the Hospital administrator had attempted to mollify the doctors with a promise to increase their pay by 15% if they returned within ten days.

By the tenth day, the angry chairman of the Hospital board, Horton Louis, unceremoniously directed Freeland to fire every one of the doctors who had left. For added measure, Louis ordered withheld any benefits the doctors might otherwise be due. He instructed the Hospital's lawyers to explore antitrust litigation to bankrupt the doctors with legal bills. With that pronouncement, Louis insisted that he personally *represent the Hospital concerning any offer to sell the clinic.*

Immediately, upon the departure of the Black doctors, the Hospital replaced the clinic physicians with doctors who before had performed administrative duties, medical students, and retired practitioners. At the same time, the Hospital placed ads in medical journals across the nation for young doctors. It offered these candidates the same 15% raise in pay it had sought to entice the Black physicians who had left.

The Hospital's position on the sale of the clinic was as aggressive as its position on the physicians who had left the Hospital. "No deal. No way!" Louis shouted at anyone who suggested compromise.

Sylvia called Dr. Boyd in the third month after the walk out. She asked how things were going. Sylvia still worked at the Medical School. She knew that the Hospital had fired the doctors who had walked out. She was aware that the Hospital would not deal with the doctors. Last, she knew that business at the clinic had been flat for several months, while the cost of providing care had increased.

Dr. Boyd was struggling without much income, trying to wait out the Hospital. Sylvia had heard that Culver had been using political contacts to pressure the Hospital into negotiating with the doctors. Yet, Louis remained a stone wall. Despite all the small talk between them putting a happy face on the situation, both Sylvia and Dr. Boyd knew that the doctors and the Hospital were at an impasse.

Sylvia mentioned to Dr. Boyd that she would like to meet with the doctor and his lawyer. That evening, Sylvia hosted her guests with her unique solution.

"How much," she pondered, "would it be worth to the doctors if most of the patients stopped using the clinic within the next two weeks?"

"I don't know," Culver mused. "It certainly would complicate the Hospital's position here. What would the people do for medical care?"

"I don't know," Sylvia offered. "Maybe they could use some of your doctors."

"Now, that's really interesting," said Culver intrigued. "Do you think we could set up a competing clinic anywhere in the Village?"

"Well," Sylvia thought. "I might be able to help you arrange a place. Of course, you'll have to take care of any zoning and government requirements. Now, let's get back to what it's worth to you?"

"Do you have something in mind, Sylvia?" Culver asked.

"Let's say that you have money on the table now. Let's say next, the patients leave the clinic. Let's say even more, that they then go to your doctors. Doesn't that make the clinic worth less?"

"I would think it makes it harder for the Hospital to hold onto its position." Culver reflected.

"Maybe you should lower your offer."

"Sylvia, that's a thought," Culver considered. "But leave the negotiating to me."

"No," Sylvia insisted, "I wasn't trying to tell you how to negotiate. I was just saying that, if you were to lower the offer, and the patients were then to stop using the clinic, and you were to lower the offer even more, and the patients were to start using the doctors, you might get them to sell for even less. If you manage that, I'd like 10% of the difference. Instead of paying all the money to the Hospital, pay just a fraction of what you save to me."

"Well, Sylvia," Culver said with a smile. "You've really taken to high stakes dealing. We'll have to think about it."

Within ten days, Culver reduced the doctors' offer for the clinic from $6,000,000 to $5,000,000. Louis only laughed at the nerve of his adversaries. He assured them that these tactics would never intimidate him into dealing anything.

A week later, patient usage at the clinic dropped 30%. By the third week, business at the clinic had been reduced to just a trickle. Louis surveyed the patient usage figures in his meeting with Freeland.

As his face reddened, Louis observed sourly, "Just cut costs. We don't need all these over priced doctors and nurses now. Reassign the surplus staff back to the Hospital."

CLAIRVOYANCE

Four months after the doctors left, the doctors reduced their offer to $4,000,000. Louis could not bring himself to laugh at this development. He could just manage a distasteful sneer, as he remained steadfast: "No deal. No way!"

Later that week, Freeland reported to Louis that the doctors who had left were seeing patients at the Village Community Center. Louis could not even sneer now. He just looked sick. Then he became suddenly flush. He was boiling to rage, and Freeland knew the signs of an imminent blow out. "Shut 'em down," the Chairman yelled to Freeland. "Call City Hall. Who owes us down there?"

It was too late. Louis had lost. Freeland knew it. He endured the blasts of Louis' anger. Then, after the Chairman was done, Freeland reasoned: "We'd best cut our losses now. This year will be a financial disaster for us if we continue to stonewall this thing. Already, the clinic has gone from cash positive to a loss leader. Already, we have seen the offer for this albatross go from $6,000,000 to $3,000,000. Soon, we'll pay them to take it off our hands. Face it, Mr. Louis. We have to accept their offer. Maybe, we can nickel and dime some concessions on Hospital admissions to save face, but it's over."

By the seventh month after the walkout, the doctors had acquired the clinic for $2.7 million. When it was over, the doctors were indebted to Sylvia for $330,000.

After discussing the situation further with Culver, she accepted a 10% interest in the venture, without having to risk her home at all. She also negotiated a favorable option agreement to purchase an additional interest in the venture. She borrowed $50,000 on her home to purchase the equivalent of another $150,000 interest in the venture on top of what she already had.

As it turned out, the patients who changed doctors got more for the change than satisfaction. Sylvia had promised every patient who changed at her request part of her share in the future venture.

At the end of its first year of operation, the clinic became again the cash producer it always had been. This time, the cash it produced was for the doctors who staffed it, the patients who used it, and for Sylvia, who came to make it all possible.

Thinking about Economic Development for African Americans

As we look ahead to the future we need our economy to make possible, we can state what we need the economy to do for us. Assessing where we are, and where we need to go to secure that future, we can also identify the kinds of things we need to do. The economy that creates our desired future must

- Support a notion of community for African Americans in which African Americans are indispensable and in control

- Allow African Americans to earn a living suitable to support families and nurture the respect of our children
- Promote the development and refinement in African Americans of those skills this economy may require from time to time
- Develop businesses owned by African Americans offering quality goods and services
- Be based on the idea that we can trust one another until we prove ourselves unworthy of trust
- Develop its relationship with other communities to secure the greatest advantage for African Americans
- Develop a base of businesses to turn dollars in the community over several times before the dollars leave the community
- Develop products unique to the community for marketing outside the community
- Create opportunities in areas requiring low capitalization, such as trading in information, distributing already made goods, or offering consumer or professional services
- Identify and develop the economic opportunities that will present themselves in the future.

A Glimpse at the Future

As we look to the future, we see a community of people earning a range of incomes, living with others of multiple generations and varied levels of education. We are joined together in an economy that enriches all of us. We have come to value education as a resource that enhances our value and marketability in an economy that enriches us for our value and our marketability.

We have educated ourselves to our economic interests. We have learned to see how money flows through our communities and how it benefits each of us. We can follow the dollar spent, from the vendor, to the supplier, to its employee, to the bank, and back to another vendor.

With each exchange of the dollar, it supports another business, pays another paycheck, makes another deposit to the account of another member of our community. We manage our own money. We attend to where we spend it, where we save it, and where we invest it. We make these decisions based upon how it benefits us.

We have discerned the value we add to our economy merely by acting as a *community*. For us, *community* is more than a word of identity or a source of pride. It is an economic resource of quantifiable value.

We have modeled that value through information we have gathered and maintained about ourselves. We have made that information a commodity. We market that information outside our community at our price to those outsiders who would partake in our prosperity with us.

We have taken the initiative to make our own economic development decisions. Associations of business people and residents work together to develop an economic strategy for the neighborhood. We have nurtured a favorable climate for at-home businesses and a marketplace of vendors to gather in one place to profit from common areas and common amenities. A community business center offers support services to the many people who have pursued their own entrepreneurial dreams.

We have created an economy that is fundamentally entrepreneurial. We long ago recognized that the greatest economic security an economy could give anyone is the security of working for yourself.

While our economy nourishes and rewards initiative, that initiative also supports a base of jobs. This work is both open and accessible to those African Americans who would work for themselves to support their own families. This work offers a real chance for progress, advancement and development to something better.

The community has its banks, its shops, its office buildings, its health care system, its lawyers and accountants. The community also has the schools it "owns" in every sense. It has religious institutions that invest in housing for people who need its boost for shelter. It elevates others who need a little more time, help, and compassion to find their place in our economy.

We have marketed our communities to other African American businesses from elsewhere in our state and beyond. We bring in natural trading partners looking to do business in the marketplace we have created with the businesses our neighbors have developed. These partnerships bring into our community new dollars and add value to our economy.

We do business with White folk. However, it is not as it once was. We no longer view it a privilege to deal for less than our value just for the fellowship with, or even approval of, others.

We bargain now. We get value now. We have alternatives now. If value is not available from the market outside our community, we have our own market to support the value we require. We can enhance our value in dealing by choosing not to deal for less than we find suitable.

The future makes us proud. This future gives us the moral authority to control our own communities, raise our own children, and set our own values simply because, in this future, we own ourselves. We are in charge of us.

We pursue that future economy along two tracks. First, we establish the economic infrastructure to create an economy that values who we are. Second, we transform what we value to realize that community of interests in which money does more than buy and sell things. In this way, it can help enrich our lives.

Building the Infrastructure of an African American Economy

Building this economy that values the contribution and participation of African Americans requires African Americans. It requires African American leadership. It requires African American financial capital. It requires African American human capital. To support the economy, the economy requires African American family and community institutions to help create an attractive environment for investment.

Any economy begins with investment. Here, investment includes all forms of contribution: money, effort, talent, tangible assets, risk of loss, and information.

CLAIRVOYANCE

What attracts any potential investor is the potential for growth. With the African American community, that climate favorable to investment in it arises when people can believe that tomorrow for it will, in tangible ways, be better than today.

Growth in the African American community presents a double-edged sword. On the one hand, conventional perceptions of its prospect are so dim that it is hard to think of anything other than decline for it. On the other hand, given this perception, it takes little to show significant growth. The growth potential for this community is almost unbounded.

First steps are often the hardest. No one will invest in the future of the African American community without the commitment of African Americans to that future. We have to believe in ourselves. We have to believe in our own future.

Yet, such has not been our recent experience in North America. Self confidence with the specificity needed to manifest value in the African American community by African Americans is new. We need an institutional support for that new confidence we must express to one another and the rest of the world.

These institutions support the values in our community. We need these same institutions to support the value of our community and the unrealized value of everyone who is a member of our community.

Our churches and mosques have undergirded us in times of assault. Our schools have attempted to elevate us through education. In our fraternities and sororities, we have found fellowship. Our community needs something else now from our institutions. It needs confirmation of our economic value.

Our community also needs economic leadership: people to take charge of the economic direction of things. We have looked to leadership in other arenas to move us to see a new vision, to develop and plan opportunities, to discern obstacles, and to identify and mobilize resources.

We need economic leadership for the same purposes. From the standpoint of our infrastructure, we need to identify the sources from which our community will nurture and develop the economic leadership it needs.

The human capital of our community is its most accessible asset. We have people of grit and determination. We also have people who are superbly trained to do things that our grandparents hardly dreamed. Yet, we are dispersed in America.

Over the last 30 years, African Americans have received the best education and training that America had to offer. Still, we are cursed to wander far and wide to find a place to showcase our talents and skills. Our best and brightest are everywhere, but not necessarily in concentration where our business opportunities are.

As refugees in corporate America, we often had little, if anything at all, to do there with all our talent and training. In that arena, people were blind to the opportunity we presented.

As mainstream firms "right sized," they have done us a favor of sorts. They make available to us to come home again the talent and ambition that left us for the specter of success. The challenge our economic infrastructure presents is how to bring African Americans of talent and training together with African Americans of unvarnished determination around the opportunities present in our own community. Here is the community of interests that enriches us all.

For this opportunity to emerge, the infrastructure requires still more components. We need an information network to make it possible for us to communicate among ourselves in our *diaspora* of talent. To take advantage of the business opportunities in our own communities, we need to confer quickly, at times over great distances.

We need communication to develop relationships among talented people around the country to promote trust, common business values, and an understanding of what people do and what they do not do. As new models for doing business with one another arise from our efforts, we will need to look to common sources for human capital, informed by the same vision of *our* economics.

Finally, our infrastructure will need to deliver the capital *where* the opportunity is present. To bring capital together in sufficient quantity to develop the opportunities in our community, we need financial institutions. These institutions include banks, credit unions, savings and loans, and other entities for assembling capital for equity, such as religious congregations, fraternities, or even not-for-profits.

As we create this capital infrastructure, its focus should be to secure an equity interest in the community's business base, as opposed to increasing the community's debt. With a financing structure geared toward equity, the community's economy is directed more toward the growth of the community's business assets than the recapture of these assets to repay debt.

As African Americans, we benefit from the growth of our business base. We are not enriched merely by the repayment of debt. The community only exchanges dollars from one pocket to another. We add no value.

The Values of a Vital Economy

The values of a vital economy are not necessarily the values we now espouse. After decades of powerlessness, having little choice but to accept a result that never met our expectations or our needs, African Americans are suffering a crisis of values and a crisis of valuelessness.

How we think about ourselves and our place in the world shapes the worth we see in what we do and what we have. Tragically, in our own eyes, what we do and what we have is worth less than what we can get from others outside our community.

The power of negative thinking goes beyond this question of value. We have accepted as inevitable that we cannot win. While winning was not an option for us economically, we still did not accept losing. What we sought instead was simply to avoid losing. We took the safe course, even to forego the opportunity for great gain.

The economic consequence of risk avoidance is limited gain, if any gain at all. In a world in which we convince ourselves that we cannot live well, we instead chose to die slow.

We have accepted that wealth is properly tied to a good job. We would rather work for a good income than own the business.

CLAIRVOYANCE

Rather than invest for great long-term gain, we save for a safe but small return. Rather than save at all, we spend to meet immediately, and with certainty, only our present needs.

We have been content to make our world small. We admire the athlete who earns millions selling athletic shoes -- principally to African Americans. Yet, we fail to see that the corporation that pays the millions to the athlete we admire makes hundreds of millions of dollars -- largely off us.

Who should we really admire then? The athlete who may take the millions or the African American businessperson who could create several times that much from his or her own daring and intelligence? The choice we make reflects the values of a community that does not value itself.

What must we do as a community to value ourselves? First, we must believe enough in ourselves to chance winning -- even to risk losing. From this standpoint, we should prefer owning to renting, profits to salary, investing to saving, and building to taking. We have to embrace the uncertainty of independence, forsaking the demeaning comfort of being cared for at the whim of someone else.

We have to think enough of ourselves to tell ourselves the truth about ourselves. We do ourselves no service to tell ourselves that we are very good when we are not. We do our neighbor no good to mislead him to believe the same about himself when his skills might be deficient or his idea might be flawed.

To be better than we are, we have to risk failure. We have to understand that failure is just temporary. It is an opportunity to learn to be better. By being better, we enhance our value and increase the return we get for marketing ourselves.

In our African American economy, excellence is value. When we allow less than our best, we diminish ourselves and the value we have.

In a world where winning was not likely, and where losing was all around, protecting those of us likely to suffer loss not only reflects compassion, it makes sense. However, once the prospect of winning becomes real, and the cost of protecting people from losing makes winning less likely, what once made sense before makes sense no longer. What once looked like compassion may no longer be.

A vital African American economy complicates our lives. It changes the world as we are used to thinking about it. It offers a new prospect that African Americans can do well if we choose. If we can transform our world to be kinder to people like us, can we easily choose to risk that transformation for anyone?

Our commitment to economic development brings with it a new understanding about how we help those who would not help themselves. In this sense, we help by creating the opportunity for any African American to do well, if he or she should choose. Our focus in an African American economy is not just to take care of people who cannot care for themselves, but to make the choice to do well a real one -- for *all* African Americans.

New Issues

Economic development for African Americans creates new issues. This idea of an African American economy, however, challenges accepted assumptions. With its focus on wealth creation and business ownership over jobs, are we being elitist? In its focus on an African American identity, are we being "separatist?" With our vision of an economy that works for those who choose to work, are we lacking compassion for those who choose differently?

These issues are largely irrelevant to African Americans. Without any economic development that works for African Americans, questions of elitism, separatism, and absent compassion are moot points.

All of us -- Black and White -- are in a world of trouble if African Americans find no way to participate meaningfully, and in large numbers, in the American economy. The least of our problems will be elitism and separatism, and we all will need for ourselves someone else's compassion. If an African American economy succeeds in bringing in numbers of African Americans to participate meaningfully in the American economy, how can it be elitist, separatist, or anything else?

Jobs have no magic for African Americans. It rings nicely in a politician's speech to pronounce that so many jobs came to this or that jurisdiction. However, who filled the jobs? What kinds of jobs are these? What opportunity for progress do the jobs offer African Americans? What will happen if the jobs move? African

American businesses, wherever they are, whatever they do, hire African Americans.

Our focus on business ownership is not a focus on owner-ship *instead* of jobs. It is a focus on ownership *for* jobs -- jobs for African Americans to build a future.

The focus on wealth creation is not just on making a few people wealthy. The focus is on making the African Americans who form a community, wherever we are, economically secure. Historically in America, that objective has never been achieved -- much less pass as elitist. Certainly, it is an achievement to be fostered, not questioned.

There is no magic in doing business with people unlike us just for the sake of fellowship. There is little profit in fellowship -- at least for the African Americans involved. Somehow, working together in the past has never overcome the separatism reflected in the allocation of fair return for the effort at the end of the day.

We now do business together when others exploit our market and our labor force. We remain separate, nonetheless, in ownership, management, and return on investment. That separatism -- whether generated by the economics of the American economy or not -- concerns few, other than the African Americans who lose out.

Perhaps, a more pointed cultural focus up front in the protection of our market results in a fairer allocation of return at the end. That "separatism" -- if it is separatism at all -- results from the economics of an economy that works for African Ameri-cans. There is no separatism other than a desire to cause a result that works for Black folk. If that is "separatism," so be it. The alternative is not acceptable to African Americans.

In any event, the "separatist" assertion miscasts the economic relationship. An African American economy is no more a separate economy than the many sectors of the mainstream economy. Its cultural focus is not to exclude others, but to assure that the points of interaction with the mainstream economy will benefit, rather than disadvantage, African Americans. The alternative is the present interaction with the mainstream economy. That interaction has not benefitted Black folk at all.

Finally, the issue of compassion is a false one. The African American community now is economically strapped to keep itself afloat, let alone take care of those people whose needs exceed their ability to care for themselves. A vital and growing African American economy can only strengthen the capacity of African Americans to care for the members of our own community -- not diminish it.

A vital African American economy is a foundation for African American community. For that community to provide identity for African Americans and to provide grounding for the values of community that will allow all of us to live together, the community must have an economy that allows African Americans to participate fully in the American economy.

That African American economy must support African American prosperity as a reality. That economy must give expression to the value of African Americans in a way the mainstream never has, and likely never will -- without the spur of an African American economic alternative. In any serious thinking about economic development, the idea of an African American economy is inevitable.

Conclusion

The focus of economic development in the African American community must be on ownership. While for many, economic participation may flow from employment, jobs alone offer limited promise for African Americans. Jobs can come and go, as people outside our community may dictate.

The jobs that count for us are the jobs we own. These jobs we keep. These jobs we build upon to make our communities something more than we found them.

The jobs we own are in the businesses we own. To create these jobs, we must create a base of businesses we own. To support that base, we need a pool of labor that offers its excellence. We need a base of investment that sees our value and undergirds that potential with the capital to realize its return for African Americans. We need a market of consumers to buy the product of our substance. We need a community of pride that accepts, as a matter of course, the value of what it produces and assures, as a matter of course, that what it produces has value.

What creates and expresses the value of who we are is our African American economy. In developing such an economy, we must do the things that other communities do to build an economy. That includes starting the businesses, investing the money, working hard to make payroll, buying for value, and saving to invest in tomorrow.

But, as African Americans, we must do more. For us, economic development is as much a question of soul, as substance. We can have access to all the capital we need. We can have arrayed all the talent necessary to build the businesses and create an economic empire managed by talented African Americans. Yet, we can fail still.

There are such people of talent now creating that economic infrastructure. They should continue to assemble the reserves of capital, identify the business opportunities, array the talent, plot the strategies, and plan the businesses.

Yet, without that transformation of the vision of Black folk to see the value inherent in all of us, we lose sight of how owning our own economy benefits all of us. We also lose the values of community that make that economy a reality. All we will ever have is the capacity to manage money. What we will lack then is its value.

Managing only money, we content ourselves with moving it from one pocket in the American economy back to another pocket. In due time, the American economy moves it back again to the mainstream -- away from us. Such has been the history of things on this continent.

Only by transforming and harnessing the souls of Black folk do we add value to the efforts of African Americans to make the rewards of our talent and risk taking inevitably our own. That value only we control. That value expands the American economy and makes the pie big enough for all Americans, especially the African Americans who expanded it, to have a satisfying share of the return.

THE WEALTH OF BLACK FOLK

Economic development for African Americans must mean more than just managing money. Managing money for African Americans has never been just managing money anyway. We must manage the value that the money only represents.

That value is the wealth of Black folk. The wealth of Black folk is grounded in the souls of Black folk. Harnessing the souls of Black folk to capture the economic power of African Americans is what economic development has to be -- for us. Any other course serves only the purposes of some other community.

The Fire that Does Not Consume:

New Thinking on Education

Most fundamental truths begin with a simple realization. For instance, we seek to help the hungry. We recognize that we can feed a person today by giving him a fish. But, we say, he will feed himself tomorrow, if we teach him *how* to fish.

Even here, there is a more fundamental truth we miss in our assumption that he is like us. Assuming that there are fish to catch, and that we are good at imparting the knowledge of *how* to fish, we still cannot teach him *why* to fish.

We assume that, with information about fishing, he will suddenly decide that it is good to fish -- because he is hungry. We say to ourselves, "Why wouldn't he fish? That is what I would do."

We forget that he is not who we are. Perhaps, the most fundamental truth about all of humanity is identity. He will always be himself, not us. If he does not know how to live independent of us, he may choose instead to die defying us -- if only to prove he is his own.

Only he can discover *why* to fish. We cannot teach him why. When he discovers why to fish, he may fish. He even may grow corn. Whatever he does, he -- not us -- chooses to do.

What he thus discovered is not how to fish or even how to grow corn. He has discovered how to live without us -- for himself. He has discovered how to live, without having to die in defiance to be who he is.

As African Americans, we must approach the subject of education with the simple realization that learning requires identity. *Why* we learn begins with understanding *how who we are makes learning important to us.*

We can provide the fuel. We can supply the tinder. We can keep the airway clear and unobstructed. We can even add a little heat. In short, we can create an environment to fire learning and to help that fire rage when lit.

We cannot supply the spark. The spark is identity. We can only trust in the underlying intelligence of our own people to find their own combustion point that sparks in them a fire to know.

To build a community committed to learning, we need not just flood our people with information. Rather, we must stoke in them a fire to consume it -- for whatever purpose they choose.

Ultimately, we learn best from ourselves. I am my best teacher. The most gifted educators are the people who have led each of us to that simple realization.

What to Do for Baraka?

by
John H. Morris, Jr.

Sylvia hung up the telephone. She was not pleased. Who was this boy demanding to speak with Sara? Her Sara was now the subject of the attentions of young men bold enough to try to flirt even with her. The thought brought a shiver down her spine.

The time had passed too fast. Sara was no longer the baby she had hovered over with her mother so many years before. Sara was now a 15-year-old sophomore at the city's engineering high school.

She apparently had become -- much to Sylvia's sudden dismay -- a young woman whom young men liked. Sylvia didn't know how she would react to these boys leering after her baby. At that moment, she felt the loss of her mother.

Sylvia needed now, more than ever, to hear her mother reassure her that everything would be all right with Sara. It had been three years since that dreary November day in 2019. Sylvia's mother had died in the same hospital her daughter played so crucial a role now as an officer and an investor.

Sylvia heard the door open. "Sara?!" she shouted. "Come up here right now."

She waited for her daughter to reach the second floor master bedroom of their Du Bois Circle home. Sylvia caught herself tapping the telephone table with her fingertip. She couldn't figure out whether she was angry or just plain scared

Before she could decide, Sara hurried in the room. Before Sara could say anything, Sylvia blurted out "Who's the boy?"

CLAIRVOYANCE

"What boy, Mama?" Sara coyly asked, pretending not to know what her mother was talking about.

"The boy who just called here, Sara," Sylvia responded. "Don't you dare pretend you don't know what I'm talking about. Who's this boy?"

"I don't know no boys, Mama," Sara pleaded. "Who you talking about?"

"You know who I'm talking about, girl. That bold thing who wanted to know whether I was as 'fy-ine as my daughter and as rich as they say.' Who's the boy, Sara?"

Sylvia clearly was angry now. Fear had long ago walked out the room.

"Oh," offered Sara. "You must have run into Baka. He's harmless."

"You'd hardly know that from his mouth," Sylvia let out, relieved that this boy seemed so unimportant to her baby. "Why's he calling here anyway?"

"We're just friends, Mama. Can I go to the movies this weekend?"

"With that clown? You can't be serious, Sara."

"Mama, we're just friends, and it's just a movie. Relax. I'll be safe with Baka."

Sara was always level headed. Since Sylvia's mother had died, it seemed that Sara had grown up a lot in Sylvia's eyes.

"O.K., Sara. He's your friend. But I want to meet him."

"If that's what you want. But, Baka is Baka. I don't think you'll get along with him at all."

Sylvia was satisfied that her daughter was more than enough for the clown she had spoken to on the telephone. It was Tuesday. She didn't give Baka a second thought until Saturday afternoon when she opened the door. Even then, Sylvia was not prepared for what she found.

He was a diminutive young man. Compact might be a better description. He seemed more the image of a fireplug with his shaved head. He was regaled in camouflage pants, scuffed combat boots, a brown and purple stripped shirt, a vest thing that looked like a flack jacket, all crowned with an imposing pair of sunglasses that might have doubled as goggles. He appeared to her to be ready for imminent insurrection, with everything but a combat blade, an automatic rifle, and an ammo belt slung over his shoulder.

Sylvia could only stand there. It took every ounce of strength in her just to lift her lower jaw that seemed to be resting heavily on her chest. She could say nothing -- only stare down at the strange being in front of her.

She heard it utter with the staccato of an automatic weapon: *"Beezcha!! I'm Baka. Here for Sara. She in? You Sylvia?"*

Perhaps, it was the shock of hearing her first name shoot up to her ears from such an angle. The shock was enough to rivet her attention on the thing. She managed just two words. "Young man." She continued to stare at him.

It seemed to both of them that the world had come to an abrupt halt. The silence lingered.

"Please . . . ," she continued, maintaining her poise. "My name to you is Ms. Forrest. Only my adult friends call me Sylvia." Sylvia made every effort to accentuate the word "adult."

"'Cuse me. I don't mean nothing by it. I'm just here to pick up Sara for the movies."

Sylvia stood in the door. Baka stood in front of her. She continued to stare at the little man. Then, she spoke yet again.

"Please," she said. "Come in. You'll have to wait for Sara. I asked her to get something for me from the Village drug store."

With that, Sylvia opened the door and motioned the boy into her home on Du Bois Circle. As the boy passed her, Sylvia noticed more than a hint of after shave and not a trace of stubble.

She continued to stare at the young man. As he entered the foyer, she spied his head moving from side to side, as if he were trying to take in all the renovations she had undertaken in her home over the years. Suddenly, this little boy seemed less imposing.

"Sit down," Sylvia invited. "Sara will be a while. Maybe we can talk, Baka. How do you know Sara?"

THE FIRE THAT DOES NOT CONSUME

Baka looked up at Sylvia. His eyes betrayed a glint of uneasiness, as if he expected someone to direct a hot light in his face and bombard him with questions he had no desire to answer. He answered each question trying to avoid the next. Sylvia pushed him further with each answer he gave.

He told her that he had grown up in New York. He had been raised by his grandmother there. After she died, he came to Baltimore to live with his aunt. They lived in public housing on the other side of town.

Baka had met Sara riding the same bus to school. She got off to go to Poly. He stayed on to go to the Ferguson School. The City had created the Ferguson School as a place for disruptive students.

The moment Sylvia heard Baka mention Ferguson, her old fear came back in the room. Who was this strange boy involved with her daughter? What was a young girl like Sara doing with him?

Again, Sylvia wanted to look to the kitchen where she always had found her mother in times of stress. As self assured as Sylvia had become, she now was on the verge of panic.

Not knowing anymore what to say to this boy she now saw destroying her daughter's life, she just breathed the question that kept going through her head. She was at the point of exasperation.

"What are you going to do with your life, boy?" She couldn't even bring herself to look at him as she spoke.

"Huh?" he uttered, surprised by the profundity of such a question. "Sylvia, . . ., uh, Ms. Forrest, I don't know. What do you think?"

What could Sylvia say to this boy she knew next to nothing about? "Oh," she groped. "Well . . ., you could finish school, perhaps a little community college, go to the service, maybe?"

"Yeah, Ms. Forrest. And then what?" Suddenly this little boy was growing, not in stature, but for some reason in anger -- at nobody in particular.

"What's the point of all that, Sylvia?" he continued, forgetting himself.

"It's so easy for you to say that here on Du Bois Circle. You have it made here, as rich as you must be. You have to see how I live. I go to school when I can. Why finish? What money will I get? What life will I have?

"The service? That's a punk's life. The army's no place for a Black man. Why risk dying for my country when I can do better risking dying for me?

"There's a world out there, Sylvia, you don't know nothin' about. There's money on the streets. You just gotta be hard enough and bad enough to pick it up. That's what I'm gonna be -- paid."

Sylvia was not prepared for this outburst. Still shaken, all she could say was her fear.

"What about Sara? Where is Sara in your world, Baka?" She said his name with a bite, as if she had bitten into a bitter pill.

"That is Sara's world, Sylvia," Baka fought back, responding to the challenge. "She's there every day, and I take care of her there. Nobody bothers Sara on the bus 'cause I'm with her."

"You like Sara then, Baka?" Sylvia asked, trying to disengage from this discussion to recover a small share of her composure.

"Sure . . ., Ms. Forrest." Baka made a point of highlighting Sylvia's last name this time.

The door opened. Sara returned. She made a special effort to hurry Baka out of the house. Sylvia was fixed in her seat, trying to remain afloat in the wake of her encounter with this tugboat of a man child.

Sara saw to it that Baka spent more time with her, at her house. Unavoidably, Sylvia had to come to terms with this disruption in her life's plans for her daughter.

Baka was there when she came home. Baka was there at dinner. Over the next several weeks, Baka and Sara were inseparable.

Sylvia had to talk to him again. This time, she had to be prepared to deal with him. She could not have this encounter at home. He was now too strong there -- with Sara as an ally. She had to get this boy to the Hospital, where she was in charge.

As Baka was leaving one Saturday evening, Sylvia called him aside. She arranged to speak with him the next Monday at the Hospital. She made it a point to tell him, *"Stop by after school and make sure that Sara's safe getting home by herself."*

That Monday, Baka came to the Vivien Thomas Memorial Hospital, just south and east of Lexington Village. Baka attracted the usual attention, what with the same camouflage pants, combat boots, flack jacket and dark goggles on top of his glistening head. The people who just happened to look up when he entered the lobby might have wondered if hostilities had broken out downtown somewhere.

As he strutted into the Hospital, Baka drew the startled glares he was used to attracting. He liked making folks feel uncomfortable in his presence.

Then he noticed a new sensation. He was starting to feel a little uncomfortable himself. This was new. Why?

He started to look around him. The more he looked, the more he wanted to see. He saw a bright, glass enclosed entryway, opening onto what seemed an endless expanse of passages, all meeting at the hub he had just entered.

It wasn't the building. He was from New York. He had been in bigger, more lavish places. He saw the people looking at him, as he wandered toward the desk where Sylvia had directed him to find her. Baka expected to see Sylvia at the desk. But she was nowhere to be seen -- except, to his astonishment, in the oversized photograph mounted on the wall.

He had paid no attention to such things before on his terrorizing visits to the world off the streets. Then, he stopped dead in his tracks when he recognized this woman whom he knew only as the mother of his 'bourgie' girlfriend.

This place was different. As he approached the desk under the information sign, he looked at the people about him. Of course, he saw the patients, the people in their everyday clothes who had come in from the streets. These people were almost all Black.

He saw the white coats and blue uniforms of the people who worked in this place. He noticed the people in the business suits, the dress shirts and ties, the dresses, suits, and skirts and blouses, all with the hospital identification pinned to their clothes. Baka had been in hospitals before. He was used to these people.

Then he noticed something different. These people, too, were almost all Black.

Baka approached the information desk. An older woman wearing a telephone headset looked up from her computer screen.

She was well groomed. Her greying hair was neatly arranged. Her jewelry accented a hint of something exotic. Baka wanted this woman to like him. She refused to give him her smile.

"Can I help you, young man?" she asked coldly and formally, just before she glanced over to the nearby

uniformed security man. Baka saw their eyes meet and felt the large man in uniform approach.

Baka spoke. "I'm lookin' for Sylvia Forrest. You know where she's at?"

The woman looked at him again, adjusting her glasses.

"Excuse me, young man. What did you say?"

Baka repeated himself. With some growing agitation and apprehension, he raised his voice.

"I says I'm here to see Sylvia Forrest. She knows I'm comin'."

The woman responded, maintaining a formality that chilled the air between them. "Wait here. I'll call her."

The uniformed security man came closer.

"Young Brother, how you doin?" the security worker asked, trying to diffuse the tension.

Baka looked at his new adversary. He saw the small crescent and star that was familiar to him on the street. He knew no Arabic. Or, he would have tried to ingratiate himself to this large man he recognized as Islamic.

He heard the woman at the desk address him.

"Young man, your name would not be, uh, . . . Baka, would it?"

"Yeah," Baka asserted with some defiance.

The woman continued on the telephone. She then turned toward Baka. For the first time, he warmed in the glow of her smile. He resisted the urge to look behind him to see who she was smiling at really.

"Baka," the woman said, smiling at him, now almost grinning. "This gentleman would be happy to take you up to see Ms. Forrest." With that, she pointed at the security man.

The woman continued. "Baka, my name is Ms. Beasley. If you ever come back to the Hospital, and you need help, come see me. This gentleman is Mr. Aziz. Follow him to Ms. Forrest's office on the 15th floor."

Aziz, too, smiled warmly at Baka. "Little Brother, come on with me to Ms. Forrest."

Baka had never been treated like this anywhere in his life. As nice as it was, he still was uncomfortable.

Baka and Aziz probed deeper and deeper into the Hospital. They moved higher and higher to Sylvia's floor. As they moved, Baka's amazement grew.

He had been a lot of places in which he had seen in one place this many Black people. He had never been anywhere as big and as nice as this place where the Black people were so obviously in charge. For the first time in a long time, Baka had nothing to say. He just looked and looked and looked.

*He left the elevator on the 15th floor. Aziz and Baka took a right, then a left, and moved down to the end of the hall to a corner office. There, they found a closed door with the name "**Sylvia Forrest, Vice President of Information.**"*

CLAIRVOYANCE

Baka's eyes ached with dryness. In his trip up from the lobby, he was so intent on seeing all he could see, he had resisted the simple urge to blink.

Aziz knocked on the door. He opened it slightly, poking his head inside. "Ms. Forrest, I've brought your young man up here to the office."

Baka heard Sylvia's voice from inside the room. "Thank you, Khalid. It was real nice of you to bring him up yourself. Please, show Baka in."

Aziz responded, smiling at Baka and gently directing him with a strong arm behind the shoulder, "Here you are Lil' Brother. Go on in. Take care of yourself. Ms. Forrest, let me know if there is anything more I can do for you."

If the Hospital was something Baka was not ready for, Sylvia's office was simply beyond his imagining. Baka just staggered in, as if he were in a dream -- after he had been slugged upside the head.

"Baka," Sylvia said, spotting that her plan had had the desired effect of numbing the boy's mouth. "Sit down over there near the window."

Baka stumbled to a large wicker chair with a bright red cushioned seat. He lost himself in the chair and lost himself again in the view of the City from Sylvia's office.

"Baka," Sylvia asked, "what are we to do with you?"

"Yes ma'am?" Baka responded almost instinctively. It never crossed his mind now even to think of addressing this force of nature before him as "Sylvia."

Sylvia offered Baka some refreshment. After a chance to eat a little, drink some, and just get used to what he was seeing, Baka recovered.

Then Baka and Sylvia just talked with one another. They spent the better part of the afternoon and early evening together just talking, as Baka watched the sun descend from Sylvia's office.

Baka talked about his grandmother in New York. In fact, as he came in the Hospital and saw Sylvia's picture on the wall, he thought about his grandmother.

"You know," Baka said, staring out the window. "When I saw your picture on the wall downstairs, I said to myself that, if there was a heaven for Grandmama, this must be what it's like.

"Grandmama wasn't from the streets, though she was street tough. She grew up in Harlem back in the Sixties and Seventies. She always told these stories about going to Columbia College and all this. She wanted to be a lawyer. She even went to law school in New York. Then she couldn't get a job.

"She had to pay back loans and stuff, and she had babies to look after later. She worked where she could, and, when there was no work for her, she learned how to live on the streets.

"You asked me 'bout school, Ms. Forrest. I know about school. Don't think it's just one of those things I'd do if only I knew.

CLAIRVOYANCE

"Grandmama did the school thing. She told us all about it. What did it do for her? She was the smartest and most schooled person I ever knew. It only made her crazy. Then it made her poor. Last, it made her dead.

"I'm not half as smart as she was. What's schoolin' gonna do for me? As soon as this semester ends, as soon as I turn 16 this summer, that's it for me and school."

Sylvia did not know what to say to him. Well, she knew what the usual arguments were. Work hard. Stay in school. Find a way to earn a living for yourself and your family. But she knew what the realities were for folks like her in a world that had nothing to offer folks like her -- even with schooling.

What could she say to the grandson of a Columbia grad who had ended in poverty supporting a family and raising her grandchildren? Sylvia hadn't even finished college herself. She just had a few computer courses at the community college after she got a GED.

Sylvia looked at this terrible child in front of her. She no longer feared him. She wanted to cry. No, not for Baka -- for his grandmother.

Not knowing what else to do, Sylvia told Baka about Lexington Village. He was shocked to learn that just 15 years before, Du Bois Circle was public housing, and that Sylvia herself was then just another tenant in public housing.

She told Baka of how the Black doctors at the Village health center took over the clinic. She told Baka how, with the help of the people in the Village, the doctors became rich men and women. She told him how the people in the Village became financially secure helping the doctors. She told him finally how, with even more daring, the group had taken over the very Hospital in which the two were now seated.

As amazing as the story was, Baka asked just two questions throughout her telling of the story. First, he wanted to know how she made out so well dealing both with the White folks who ran the Hospital before and with these doctors who then took over.

Sylvia took Baka in her confidence. "Well," she began. "I did it with this." Sylvia left her chair by the window and walked over to her computer terminal.

Baka was puzzled. "How did that computer have anything to do with giving you the ice to do this takeover? What did you do, fence stolen computer equipment to raise money?"

"No, Baka," Sylvia said, shaking her head and laughing. "Come over here. Don't say another word. Just look and listen to me."

With that, Sylvia turned up the screen, punched a few keys, and called up a display.

"See that, Baka." Sylvia motioned, pointing to the flickering lines of text on the screen. "There on the

screen is the display that will tell me anything I need to know about the Hospital's patients.

"I worked for the Medical School years ago, loading data into its computer network. Well, with a little initiative, I figured out how to get into the old clinic's data base on the patients in the Village who used the clinic.

"I downloaded the data, played with it some, and found who were the most frequent and the most profitable patients for the clinic. I then got these people to agree not to use the clinic and come with the Black doctors. Most of these people were close friends of my mother anyway, and persuading them was pretty easy."

"Ms. Forrest, I don't know much about computers, but isn't that kind of stuff against the law? Didn't you just steal your way into this office?"

"Well, Baka. What I did was wrong. If I had been caught, I could have gone to jail. But the hard work that got me in here wasn't against the law. The information I got just saved some time.

"I could have done this without it really. So, I took a chance I didn't need to take the chance I had to take.

"You should understand that the real chance I took was not getting this information. It was taking on the people I worked for. If I lost, do you think I would be anywhere near here with anything to my name?"

Baka said nothing. He just looked at Sylvia. He thought to himself, "This lady has a lotta nerve gettin' on me for how I get mine on the streets. She got hers any way she could."

He kept thinking about it. The more he thought, the more he thought of Sylvia. He just wasn't sure what he admired about her more: that she stole her way to wealth or that she made it taking on the White folks in charge.

Then Baka asked, "Who is this Vivien Thomas person anyway? The wife of some rich White guy who gave you money? Is that why you named the Hospital after her?"

Sylvia could not suppress her laughter. "Baka, Vivien Thomas was a man. He died long before I was born.

"He was a Black man who worked at Johns Hopkins Hospital. He was a talented man who worked with the surgeons there. One of the things he did was help design a procedure that allowed doctors to operate on a baby's heart to save the life of the baby.

"The White doctor who worked with him became world famous. Not too many people even heard about the Black man who made the operation possible. That's why some of the doctors who took over the Hospital here wanted to name it after Mr. Thomas. They wanted to make what he accomplished as important to folks like us, so we would continue to do important things ourselves."

Baka had never heard of Vivien Thomas. As he heard Sylvia tell his story, he thought that this place really must be the heaven his grandmother went to.

"Baka," Sylvia said, as though she was about to give him some bad news. "I don't want you to drop out of school. You're Sara's friend. Maybe you'll become more than that, maybe not.

"But there is going to be some young woman, you're going to have to provide for."

Sylvia bit her lip. More than anyone perhaps, Sylvia knew what she had just said presumed a lot. But she proceeded anyway to reach Baka with flattery aimed to puff up his importance. The lesson in reality, however, would have to await another day. She had to reach him now with a different message.

"I don't know what you saw with your grandmother. Just give yourself the chance she gave herself. Just maybe you make out better.

"Don't say anything yet. Let me propose this to you. Come work for me this summer after school is over. When the summer is done, make your decision then."

"What kinda job you talkin' 'bout, Ms. Forrest? I just don't see no chance comin' outta deliverin' mail or gettin' somebody's coffee."

"Do you trust me, Baka?" Sylvia asked.

"O.K., I'll give you a chance to prove me wrong if I say I want to trust you."

"Leave it to me, Baka. Let me call you a cab to take you home." With that, Sylvia reached for the telephone on her desk and called for Aziz to take Baka back down to the lobby and to get him a cab.

As Baka left, Sylvia called out, "I'll see you back in this office the day after school ends. By the way, I don't think there's much of a chance that a war will break out here at the Hospital. Don't wear the boots, the camouflage pants, the flack jacket or the goggles. You'll do fine even with basketball shoes, jeans, and a regular shirt."

Baka worked the next summer at the Hospital with Sylvia. When he started, he asked her if she could show him how he could make money using the computer the way she had.

Sylvia turned Baka over to her director of information services. She asked him to teach Baka the highways and byways of the various data networks most in use at the Hospital.

From time to time, she and Baka continued their afternoon and evening talks. Too soon the summer ended.

The Friday before Labor Day, Sylvia heard a knock at her office door. Baka entered with a small bag under his arm.

"Ms. Sylvia," Baka began. He had taken to the old affectation of calling Sylvia "Ms. Sylvia."

Somehow, as their relationship unfolded over the summer, the formality of "Ms. Forrest" made absolutely no sense. There was now no way in the world he could ever again call her "Sylvia" -- even if he were suddenly to age 50 years.

"This is my last day. I'm about to leave. Before I go, I want to talk to you about a few things. First, thank you for everything you did. Second, I would really like you to use my real first name, Baraka.

"Baka is just what everybody calls me -- everybody but my grandmother. I was always Baraka to her.

"Here, this is a gift to you," Baka said, handing the bag to Sylvia.

She opened the bag and found a stapled collection of papers from the Hospital's laser printer.

"What's this?" Sylvia asked, staring at Baka.

"It's my best work this summer." Baka focused his eyes on the tips of Sylvia's sandals. He could not now bear to peer into her face.

"This looks like a play. It's called The Slave. You mean to tell me that you wrote this play, Baka?"

"No, Ms. Sylvia. I found the play. I also found a little of me I didn't know."

"So, you found this play, read it, and liked it. Is that why you want to make it a gift to me?"

"No ma'am." Baka quietly said. "Well, yes ma'am, to some of that. I found the play, and I read the play, and I liked the play. But that's not just why I want you to have it. I found the play and remembered the play. My grandmother used to read it to us all the time when I was real young. She'd act out the parts for us.

"When I found the play, I remembered something she said about me. She told me once about what happened to me when I was born.

"It seems that my daddy knew the streets too. His name was Leroy. My mama was in love with him. You know, the way I hope Sara feels about me. But, when I was born, and she saw I was a boy, she wanted to name me after my daddy. Grandmama was against it.

"Mama and Daddy and Grandmama had this big fight about what my name would be. My parents wanted Leroy. Grandmama couldn't stand the name. She said, 'No grandson of mine is going to be just another Leroy in this White man's world.'

"She then worked it out. She said, 'if it's got to be Leroy, don't make him no damn ordinary Leroy. Call the boy Baraka so he can be something special.' She told me that they worked out the argument to call me Baraka, and that it meant I was to be special.

"I never understood what she meant until this summer. When I was playing around in the network, I put my real name in an info search and looked at what it showed.

"I found the play you have, some other plays, some poetry and some books. I remembered all of them from Grandmama. Only I didn't know who wrote them.

"The man who wrote that play was named Amiri Baraka. His last name is my first name. Grandmama loved all he wrote.

"I looked him up some more. I found out that his name used to be LeRoi Jones, until he changed it. Just like my daddy's first name.

"But Grandmama didn't want no ordinary Leroy, so she named me Baraka, after her favorite writer.

"I then read the stuff this summer. I like it. I read some more. Now, I'm reading other writers."

"Thank you," Sylvia intoned. "You know, I've never heard of Amiri Baraka. I've never read anything he wrote. Actually, I don't read much. If you think I'll like this, I'll make it a point to read it. Maybe, we can talk about it later. Maybe you can help me understand it."

"Ms. Sylvia," Baraka said, looking down at his shoes. "I really want to thank you for this summer. I don't know if you can understand what it meant to me. I also will thank you even more if you get the Hospital to cover the bill I know I ran up finding and reading all this stuff.

"Well, Ms. Sylvia," Baraka said. He was again looking at his shoes -- not just because he was wearing the first pair of dress shoes he had ever owned. He was stalling for time -- to avoid telling her his decision.

Then, he just blurted it out. "I can't go back to Ferguson now. Even if I could, I couldn't go to Poly with Sara. More now than ever, there's nothing at Ferguson for me. And, I won't punk for nobody going to school with all those smart asses -- even to be in school with Sara.

"If I could know everything I needed to work here, I'd stay to work that computer. But I know that there's no place for me here."

Baka's voice trailed off. There was just silence. He stood in front of Sylvia motionless, staring at the carpet in front of him. Suddenly, he showed a trace of agitation. With no sign of warning, he broke the silence, muttering almost under his breath, "I gotta go."

Still looking down at his shoes, Baraka executed a balletic spin and left Sylvia's office. In the span of no more than a moment, he was gone.

After she noticed that he was gone, Sylvia futilely called out to him. "Baraka. I'm sorry you have to leave. Take care of yourself." But there was no one to hear her.

Sylvia sat alone in her office, as she watched the sun set out her window. It had been more than three hours since the young man she met what seemed a lifetime ago had left her office.

She reached over to her phone and punched out the number of the Hospital's president. He had just returned home from the office for the Labor Day weekend. She convinced him to delay his plans for a couple of hours to meet with her on a problem that could not wait and which had to be solved.

They had to do something for Baraka.

What to Learn For

What may drive me to know more than I do may not drive you. What you find compelling to learn may not move me at all. We are different, you and I. The things that work for you to do the things you do need not work for me.

We proceed with learning as if we are all the same. If what works for you does not work for me, you assume that there must be something wrong with me.

As African Americans, we often ask the same questions about why we learn and how we learn that other people framed for themselves -- not us. When the answers we draw from those questions do not work for us, we look at ourselves for the deficiency.

Perhaps, we are not asking the right questions. Perhaps, the questions that others ask we cannot. Perhaps, what made those questions the right questions for others is that they framed those questions to suit themselves -- and their purposes. To change the outcome to find success for us, maybe we should ask the questions we frame to suit our purposes.

We take learning for granted. That is not just to say that we do not pay enough attention to questions of education. It is to say that what I may assume about my learning often is of little help to anyone else but me. As African Americans, what other people generally assume about education may be of little help to us.

We look at learning as if learning means the same thing to everyone. We look at ourselves and often forget what makes us different.

As with that hungry person we thought we might teach to fish in the opening discussion, we assume that the value of learning is self evident. Instead, each person must discover that value for himself. It is discovering why learning is valuable that gives the answer meaning.

We cannot define that value for anyone. He must discover that himself if any value at all is to be had. If we try to discover it for him, we deny him both the value and the education.

Such has been our handicap in assigning to others the shaping of our education. Such has been our advantage when we have taken on that burden ourselves.

As African Americans, we cannot learn from an education that is not our own from its most fundamental assumptions. Its assumptions must be our assumptions if learning is to be sparked.

Some of us have been fortunate to escape the consequences of other people's assumptions about education to find our own purposes in it. Others in our community have not.

As a community, our challenge is to make the value of learning discoverable by people like us, each for his own purpose. In that discovery is the education we need as a community. That discovery is the spark that ignites a fire in us that never consumes us. It only gives us power.

We assume that what other people say that makes learning valuable to them is what should make learning valuable to us. They say, for instance, that learning is power. They say it expands our world. They say it makes it possible for us to get a good job and make a place for ourselves in the world.

CLAIRVOYANCE

We take what they say at face value. Perhaps, we stop listening to ourselves.

We may not see that those who say learning is power also seem to have power whether or not they are learned. Those who say learning expands their world also have the means to enjoy the world's expanse whether or not they can learn a single new thing about it. Those who say that learning leads to a good job and a place in the world often manage to get the job and find their place without the degrees that only we seem to cherish.

As African Americans -- even those of us with the trappings of the world's success -- must confess, such learning, as others would have it, is not power. Such learning does not expand a world resistant to opening itself to people like us. Such learning leads to no job and to no place in a world unlearned in the talents and abilities of people like us.

Without clear understanding of our purpose, whatever we say about the value of learning rings hollow, because the world makes what we would say so much a lie. Yet, African Americans who see the world -- and may even detest it -- still can embrace learning. What for?

As African Americans, if we are to value learning, it can only be to change the world that makes a lie of so much we would otherwise say that makes learning valuable. We have to transform what others may say about the value of learning to reflect our own predicament.

They say learning *expands* our world. We must understand that learning can *transform* that world to work for us.

They say learning leads to a better life, a job, and a place in the world. We must see that learning leads to our discovering what is valuable in us, to our extracting that value for us, and to helping us define and obtain for us both the world we want and the place in it we choose for ourselves.

They say that learning is power. But for us, the only power we can have is the power to change a world that would deny us power. Learning can be that power -- if only we let it, and if only we refuse to deny ourselves or let others deny us.

Learning changes things. It changes how we see ourselves. It changes how we see one another. It changes how we see the world. It changes how we want our world to work -- for us.

Learning is power only if it frees us to think for ourselves. Then, we are free to change ourselves and the world in our own minds, where nothing should defeat us.

We can thus begin the hard work of creating a world that works for us. The world we create can work simply because we can convey its idea to others who may share our ambition and can strengthen ourselves against those who do not.

Learning fuels a more fundamental power. It helps me define who I am in a world so insistent on defining me for its purposes.

Learning is this ultimate power to resist the limitations the world would impose on me. It makes me able to tell the world who I am, what I do, why it is valuable, and why I must be in charge of me.

What then do we say about the value of learning? Learning, for us, is a means to an end. That end is not limited to raising test scores or increasing graduation rates or reducing the number of dropouts.

That end is the community we have been conceiving in this series. It is a community for African Americans in which African Americans do as they choose and choose as they would.

To have such a community, we need people committed to learning as we would have it. For us, learning is whatever helps us to discover

- who we are
- what we do
- why what we do is valuable
- what opportunities exist for us in the world to be who we would choose
- what we must do to achieve our own purposes.

What Learning Must Become

Just saying the "what for," as we have here, changes how we see education. Learning becomes simply the community's process for passing on to one another the skills and values that make community possible. These values include:

- caring
- discipline
- exploration
- a sense of understanding
- a sense of reward
- a sense of wonder

- critical thinking
- knowledge.

What that community provides its members, both materially and in other ways, in autonomy and support, is the payoff we all are looking for.

We reflect upon education. We often ask what to teach. We rarely consider what makes us learn. Teaching without learning is useless. Learning without purpose is pointless. Soon, without purpose, learning becomes irrelevant to anyone's purpose until learning ceases altogether.

It is the community then that gives learning purpose. It nurtures the values that make the point of learning meaningful. It gives a place to people to find who they are. It provides support to help them make that conception of who they are real and valuable to them. The means both for that realization and the community that makes it possible is learning -- as we would define it for ourselves.

Learning thus becomes a process too important to the community to leave it in the schools, a few hours out of just half the year's days. The things the community needs are so funda-mental that these needs are not met by the subject focus of a single curriculum.

For the community we want, what must we learn? As we see it, for us to do the things we need for community, we must develop in us the following skills or attributes:

- reading/communication
- analytic thinking with words and ideas
- quantitative thinking with numbers and related concepts

- negotiation skills
- research/information development skills
- creativity
- peer resistance/influence
- group living
- an understanding of success for our own purposes
- decision-making
- option creation
- conflict resolution
- leadership/followership.

Beyond developing these skills and attributes, our new community will need to support the following values:

- identity and pride
- power/mastery/creativity
- judgment
- cooperation/power
- self-actualization
- autonomy
- choice
- hope
- self-esteem.

In reflecting on these skills and values, one reality is clear. People possessing such skills and embodying such values will not just be capable of learning. They will be anxious to learn anything they choose for any purpose they desire for themselves.

Subject matter and curriculum may be largely irrelevant. Where people secure those skills and embrace those values is not in any school or from any textbook.

The skills and values we have associated with our conceived community are not taught in schools. They are acquired by living a productive life.

Igniting the Spark of Learning

Learning is likened to the process portrayed in the film *The Karate Kid*. There, a young man wanting to learn karate, as he would have it, is taught a valuable lesson, without knowing it, in the discipline of the sport.

He has been saved from a beating at the hands of bigger and tougher classmates by an apartment janitor who knows karate. Seizing upon this fighting skill as his salvation from the other boys looking to beat him up, the young man prevails upon the janitor to teach him.

The boy eagerly accepts the janitor as a teacher of karate. Only, it seems, the janitor has other intentions. First, he has the boy wax all of the old cars he owns. He specifically instructs the boy to use a special stroke to apply the wax and then to wipe it off: "Wax on/ Wax off."

Next, he has the boy paint the wooden fence around his home. Again, he instructs the boy how to apply paint to the fence in deliberate vertical strokes.

Last, he has the boy sand his wooden floors. Again, he instructs the boy how to sand, using a deliberate stroke to do it.

While the boy eagerly awaits his karate lesson, he does these chores as a favor to his teacher. Soon, his frustration mounts.

He suspects that he is just being taken advantage of by the janitor to get free work.

At the moment his frustration and anger erupt, the boy is about to give up altogether. He voices his accusation directly to the janitor. The janitor explains that he has been teaching him karate all along.

The janitor then demonstrates the point. He walks through a number of attacks on the boy, and, using the techniques he taught, "Wax on/Wax off," "Paint the fence," and "Sand the floor," the boy fends off the attack. As the attacks intensify, the spark of realization ignites in the boy that he is beginning to master something he never before thought he could do.

Later in the film, the boy proceeds on his own to develop and train himself in a special technique the janitor just mentioned to him. It is that technique the boy uses, at the end of the film, to win the karate championship.

The film is, in many respects, an allegory of learning. As it was with the young man, so it is with each of us. We are eager to reap the benefits of knowing what we would, but do not, know. We, however, loathe doing the things we need to do in order to master the skills that produce the benefit.

Like the boy, we nonetheless learn. We have those special teachers in whom we repose the trust -- or the fear -- to do the things we must do to acquire the skills we need. We find the discipline that skill requires. We also are fortunate to find the payoff that it produces.

If we are particularly thoughtful, we learn another valuable lesson about learning. Learning transforms us.

What we first thought the payoff was may not be what we ultimately find valuable in the learning. For the young man, the initial value was being able to beat up his attackers. What he ultimately found, however, was something in himself that he did not know before was there.

This allegory offers us useful insights. We cannot compel or convince someone else to learn. The process of learning produces its own rewards that we cannot predict. Whatever makes learning valuable, the person has to discover for himself or herself. Learning changes who we are and what we want in ways we cannot predict.

All we can do is create the opportunities for that discovery to happen for as many people in our community as we can manage. This discovery often does not happen at school and often happens despite school.

There are no tests given in self discovery. There are no special curricula for people to find their own joy in learning. The only proof of such discovery is our personal commitment to accomplish something we before never thought we could do. Such things could be as modest as balancing our own check book or reading the books of our choosing, or even as ambitious as inventing the next system of thinking that changes the world.

We see several simple steps in this process of learning. First, like the boy, we must have some underlying trust, faith or fear in our instructor. We then do the things we need to do that we may not yet understand that make understanding possible.

Often, the things we must do are the things we do not want to do until *after* we understand their value. We never get that understanding without first doing things we do not want to do. Thus, key to this process of learning is the relationship to the people and institutions who would spur us to our self discovery.

Next, we need to acquire the skills that would benefit us. Usually, with skill there is discipline.

Finally, we require a pay off to spark our realization that all our hardship was worth it in the end. That payoff usually is not what we expected it to be when we first embarked on this journey of discovery.

What supports our discovery of our own potential is our relationship with people who help us see that potential. These people do not let up on us as we seek to avoid the hard work of realizing it.

For many of us, these people were our mothers and fathers, grandparents, aunts and uncles. They may have been family friends or, very often, the teachers who once terrorized our after school thoughts.

The community we now face is unlike the community of our fond memories. For many people in our community, the mothers and fathers do not share the same unshakable faith of our parents that education would make their children's lives better. Indeed, the community has to work mighty hard to take that idea seriously. There simply are now too few of the nurturing relationships at home or at school, like the ones that had supported our dreams when many of us were young.

If the world of our community has changed, then how we go about learning, too, must change. Otherwise, we will just waste our time trying what used to work and no longer will.

To ignite learning in the world we face, we then have to focus on where the people are who need to have their fires stoked. We have to consider how to change the environment to make it conducive to sparking learning. Then, we have to reach the people to forge new relationships to spark discovery.

Structuring the Community to Learn

For our community, learning requires the following pieces beyond schools and text books:

- Places where learning can occur. These *venues of learning* are areas where the community has sanctioned the intervention of instruction.
- Activities out of which skills emerge and values arise.
- Opportunities to apply the skills and attributes developed.
- Recognition and reward for achievement.

When we think of our own experiences, we had two places that nurtured in us the desire to know more than we already knew: our homes and our schools. Today, our relationships at home and in school are not strong enough to pass on the learning we need.

We need to expand these nurturing relationships throughout the community. We need to free the community to make itself an expanded *venue for instruction* in the things the community needs.

Our relationships range from the most impersonal -- the strangers we meet on the street -- to the most familiar -- the families with whom we have lived. Between these extremes lay a host of other relationships:

- at the school we attend for only 6 hours of half the days of the year
- with the neighbors who see us come and go through the neighborhood
- with the people who join us in worship
- with the coaches and volunteers we find at recreation centers or on neighborhood teams or at youth clubs
- at the barbershops, the hair salons, the corner stores where we hang out with our friends
- on the jobs we go to every work day and deal with the people who work with us
- at the clubs to which we belong that give us social identity.

All these places are now *venues of instruction* that are not working well enough to create the kind of community that works for all of us.

We must ask of these *venues* what they should now teach us about community. Do we learn in these *venues* the values and skills that will make our community work for us? Can we change what we do in these venues to promote the values we need to foster and to help us develop and sharpen the skills we need to prosper?

There is a range of things we can do to make the community a place that stokes in people the fire to know. First, we must consciously go about promoting the value of learning, as we would define it for our own communities.

Certainly, it is hard to imagine any African American having trouble getting behind such ideas as identity, pride, power, cooperation to benefit Black folk, real choice, hope, self-actualization or self-esteem. However, we must then move people to take one step beyond that: to take these matters personally.

How often during a month, because "it's none of our business," do we let pass, without saying a word, things terribly inconsistent with identity, pride, power, cooperation to help Black folk, self-actualization, choice, hope, and self-esteem? We talk about taking back our community. The first step is as simple as seeing that the community belongs to all of us, and we belong to it.

That vision requires us to understand how, in that community, the things you do, as your business, can also hurt me, cost me, limit me, or cause me to lose an opportunity. By the same token, we must see one another as vehicles for helping ourselves in ways that command our respect for one another and our faith and trust in the success of one another.

Such vision has nothing directly to do with schools or learning. It is, however, necessary to produce people who share the values of community. Among these values is a trust and belief in the power of learning to create new possibilities for people -- even people like us.

To secure these new possibilities, the community can structure for its people places where they can develop themselves. These venues include:

THE WORKPLACE AND BUSINESS

- With EMPLOYEE ASSISTANCE PROGRAMS ("EAP"), employers now address many problems that employees may have, from drug dependence to depression. As employers seek to develop their work force, learning, both as it may relate to the job and otherwise, benefits all parties. Such an expansion of the focus of these programs also provides a business opportunity for people who can provide such instruction for a price.

- With APPRENTICE/INTERNSHIP PROGRAMS, the community's businesses can become an active stakeholder in the development of its future workforce. Its businesses can give young people the chance to apply the skills they have and receive important recognition in pay, as well as in acceptance and approval.

- With MENTORING AND STAFF DEVELOPMENT to advance people and even encourage them to leave the business at some point to go on their own or with a larger operation, community businesses only improve their own business climate. As a result, they foster greater cooperation in the community's business and may develop, from their own personnel, their future suppliers or trading partners, having some measure of personal loyalty to them and their businesses.

THE NEIGHBORHOOD

- RECREATION CENTERS, LIBRARIES, SCOUTING, AND SPORTS TEAMS, and other organized youth activities, provide more or less captive audiences of young people to shape and enforce the community's values, as well as chances to apply the skills and attributes acquired elsewhere.
- LEARNING CENTERS. Learning Centers represent a non-sports analogue to Recreation Centers. They form a cross between a recreation center and a library. They create a place where young people can pursue learning in a more frivolous way. Young people can do homework and play. They can use computers, view movies, play video games, work on long-term school projects, explore science with lab equipment, experiment with electronics, perform drama, or play games that, like chess, can help develop thinking and planning skills. Here, adults willing to affirm who these young people can become and what they can do, create the bonds that spark interests beyond everyday possibilities.
- COMPUTER CLUBS OR CENTERS. These more focused learning centers can serve as a means by which the community can make the world of information accessible to its members. It can be used for homework or, by adults, for home budgeting, word processing, or even home business. The Computer Center can be a place where both young and old can come together around learning. It can also provide an opportunity, particularly for young people, to develop an understanding of, and expertise in, computing from the chance just to play

around consistently with the machines. Area businesses or computer manufacturers would benefit from contributing computers to these centers. With their contributions, these manufacturers can develop an emerging market among those African Americans who now could not afford a computer but who likely would, as they mature and develop.

INSTITUTIONS OF HIGHER LEARNING

- SATELLITE ASSOCIATION WITH AREA SCHOOLS. For young people developing toward college, early association with these institutions enhances their development and provides opportunities to them for special recognition and reward.
- SATELLITE ASSOCIATION WITH NEIGHBORHOODS. These institutions need not limit their affiliation to enrolled students. Their active presence at the neighborhood level removes the distance that may exist for people around issues of education. It also gives the institution a chance to support, recognize, and reward the achievement of people outside the formality of schooling. These institutions can then develop and tap, for themselves, the community's best talent.

These *venues for instruction* exist outside the schools. They are not intended to replace schools. Rather, they best function to support what goes on in the schools, by making what the schools do more valuable to the community.

As what happens outside the schools achieves some measure of success, that success then changes what the schools do and can do. For a long time, we have structured our learning entirely around the schools.

Then, issues arose, beyond teaching reading, writing, and figuring, that affected the ability of students to learn. In keeping with our school-focused approach, we imposed the responsibility for these complex issues upon the schools as well.

Whether or not the schools can do these things that nurture learning, we must ask whether sparking learning best rests with the schools alone. We think not. Indeed, without the active involvement of the community, it may be near impossible for the schools to spark learning at all.

We propose making our communities into true *communities of learning*. Here, the responsibility for learning rests where it was when we succeeded in sparking our desire to learn: with those closest to the student -- whatever his age.

Unfortunately, despite however many hours our teachers may spend with our children, our children do not view themselves as close to their teachers as we may have viewed ourselves to the teachers of our memory. Just as unfortunately, for many of our children, there are fewer positive forces in their lives stoking their fires and more distractions dampening their ardor. However good the schools might become, they may never be up to the task at hand.

Only the community provides a place where the value of learning can be made real to people who doubt its worth to them. It can provide those *venues* where everyone, rich and poor, old and young, can be engaged in the lifelong pursuit of learning as each would decide for himself and for his purpose. Only in community does this human collaboration in self discovery convey its own legitimacy for whatever people choose for themselves, together with their families, friends, and neighbors.

Only the community can provide recognition and reward having meaning to its own young people. Whether that recognition is expressed through signs, bumper stickers, advertisements, public campaigns for learning, or payment for achievement, the community must convey its unequivocal and unqualified message that learning matters, and that it never ends.

Continuing Thoughts

If this community-based model for learning changes the things we look for schools to do, then we must consider more at length what we want the schools to do. We also must address what we do not want schools to do.

The community structure provides its own set of benefits to the community. Some are quantifiable and translatable to money. Other benefits are not.

All these things carry costs. How does the community finance its learning? That question is larger than how it pays for its schools. Learning exists outside the schools. How does the community pay for all the things it must do to develop the people it will need to build for it a better future than past?

As we conceive that structure of schools and *venues of instruction*, how do we manage that complex structure so that we get the result we want? How do we define, as a community, the result we want? Certainly there is no standardized testing to tell us that answer. Still, we must set for ourselves the benchmarks we must hit if we are to be successful in achieving the result we want.

Finally, this structure, this community, this goal of learning for our purposes exists only in the minds of people bold enough to conceive it. It clearly does not exist in the world of lowering expectations and frustrated needs we now face. How then do we begin the hard work of making this wonderful dream a working reality?

Finding Ourselves in the Child

How do you move a community to embrace its potential? How do you establish this "community of learning" we spoke of in **The Fire That Does Not Consume** to carry us, as African Americans, into a proud and prosperous future?

Such was the objective we set for ourselves when we reexamined questions of learning and education for African Americans. The question we must pick up now is how do we begin.

For us, that beginning rests in ownership. By ownership, we mean that responsibility for something that only results from exclusive and unqualified possession of it.

Ownership is that which makes the thing precious to me mine. For us, the most precious of the possessions entrusted to us are our children. To exercise "ownership" in this sense, we must assume responsibility for their development.

As these beings are the most precious of the possessions entrusted to us, should we neglect their development, we then are capable truly of "owning" nothing. In this sense, learning and education in our communities become necessary elements of our ever "owning" anything -- including ourselves.

If we do not "own" the education of the children our communities produce, can we own anything in the community? Indeed, can we even say we have a community?

As we build this "community of learning," we begin with the child. We create for the child a world that offers to the child the *reality* of all the child can accomplish.

A community makes the potential of its children real by surrounding them with the chance to become whatever each child wants to be. More significantly, it gives its children the chance to become whatever they may never have dared to dream.

We do that by arraying the opportunities the community has to offer to make them available to the child. When we do that for the child, we also do it for ourselves. In this sense, with our focus on the child, we find ourselves in the child -- as we find again the child in ourselves.

Planting the Future Seed:
Preparing a Community Harvest

by
John H. Morris, Jr.

Even though she was a big deal at the Hospital, Sylvia still walked to work. Among the joys of living in Du Bois Circle were her morning and evening walks to and from her office.

Sylvia thrilled in the cold wind that stung at her face as she trudged through the March snow. It reminded her of being alive. It also carried her to times past when she was a little girl, walking hand in hand with her mother to the bus stop. She recalled when her role changed, and she walked with Sara through the cold. In that private reverie, she warmed herself in the glow of memory.

Sylvia approached the Hospital. Across the street, she saw the young people going through the daily ritual of pushing and shoving one another until the bus arrived to cart them off to school.

Today, strangely, the children held her notice. She stopped at the corner, waiting for traffic to clear. The cars and the trucks sped by, kicking up, as they passed, blackening coals of ice that hurled themselves at Sylvia. She never moved. She never saw them.

She kept watching the little men and women showing off for one another. She saw how young they were. She sensed how little they knew of the world. She felt how the world was too much with them far too soon.

For the first time in her life, Sylvia was disconnected from the future. Whatever would be would have little to do with her. It would have a lot to do with them -- these lost children in front of her.

For the first time in her life, she thought about the future with the fear of having no control. At that moment, she began to tingle with the hardening of her own arteries. For the first time in a long time, she thought of Baraka.

It had been six months since he left her office the Friday before Labor Day. She had not seen him for that time. Sara had not heard from him at all. It was as though he had dropped off the face of the earth.

CLAIRVOYANCE

Sylvia looked out at these children toying innocently with the bear of a world they poked and prodded. She knew that with just the slightest movement when aroused, this bear they taunted could disable and devour them -- and all her hopes for her Sara.

She had to know that Baraka would make it. She had to believe that somehow even Baraka could outwit the bear, as she had managed.

Months ago, she had tried to work out a way for Baraka with the Hospital president. It was, however, her embarrassment that, after three lengthy conversations on the subject of what to do for Baraka, when it finally came to doing something, Baraka was no where to be found.

The quiet of the street awoke her from her thoughts. Sylvia hurried across the intersection. She went straight through the Hospital lobby, barely acknowledging the friendly faces greeting her. She rode the elevator to the 15th floor. Then, moving directly to her office, she shut the door without saying a word.

Without bothering to take off her long down coat, she walked to the telephone on the left side of her desk. From memory, she punched the extension.

"Dorothy," she smiled into the telephone, "can you do me a favor? I know you tried this back in September, but I need you to track down Baraka for me. Find what you can."

Sylvia sank down in the big soft leather chair behind her wood veneer desk. She stared out her window at the snow that still choked the city streets beneath. Then, looking at the stack of papers on her desk, she got up, took off her coat, placed it on the hanger behind her door, and calmly lost herself in the day's work.

After lunch, while Sylvia was pondering a small logistical problem that had occupied her that entire morning, her telephone interrupted her determined effort at distraction. She touched the button to turn on her speaker and, without attending, answered the call.

"Ms. Forrest," the voice on the other end intoned. "I think you want me to speak to you about this."

In her distraction, Sylvia did not recognize the voice of the woman she had given what had seemed so important an assignment just hours before. "O.K.," Sylvia offered. "Well, who is this?"

"It's Dorothy Stewart, Ms. Forrest. Remember, you asked me to track down Baka. Well, I think I found something that you might find interesting. You'll want to have Ronny join us, I think. Can I come up right now?"

"Of course," Sylvia responded. "I want to see you immediately. Let Ronny know I want to see him, too."

Ron Hammond was the Hospital's director of information services. The previous summer, Sylvia had turned Baka over to him to learn the byways of modern information services. As she waited for the messengers to deliver the information she so much wanted to hear, she began to think about what might be so interesting.

CLAIRVOYANCE

Sylvia was not long in waiting and not at all disappointed. It was quite interesting. It seemed that Baka's Hospital computer authorization was still active. The account had generated about $26,000 in charges -- since Baka had left.

Without waiting to hear anything more, Sylvia exploded, "What's going on here, Ron!?"

"Sylvia, believe me, it's not as bad as it looks." Ron was starting to squirm under the swelter of Sylvia's glare.

"For your own sake, Ron, and for mine, I hope it's not as bad as it looks. I trusted you with Baka. Don't let me down with something that'll send all of us to jail."

"Hold on, Sylvia," Ron assured. "Everything's under control. The Hospital has every dime of those charges covered. I can call accounting to show you that there is no deficit showing in the department."

"Well, Ron, if the Hospital didn't cover the charges, who's fronting for Baka on this? Is it you? You're nuts if you're advancing that boy money like this!

"Sylvia," Ron said, lowering his voice, "brace yourself now . . . . I don't have to front for Baka. He's covering these charges himself."

"I'm no fool, Ron. How'd you let yourself get involved in this? Where legitimately could Baka get money like that? As of this minute, we do nothing more for Baka. You got that?"

"Sure, Sylvia. If that's what you want. But, I assumed that this was all right with you. He was your boy and all last summer."

"Ron, how'd Baka work the access, the billing and the payments?"

"Well," Ron began, "Baka called me up late last September, asking for his old access number for the various databases we use. He said he could pay and pay up front. So, based on an arrangement to pay as he went, I gave him the number and kept it open as long as he paid. He started with an up-front payment of $2,000. He has this post office box where we send a bill each week, and each week we get a money order in the mail."

"When did you get the last money order?" Sylvia probed.

"'Bout five days ago," Ron relayed offhand. "We're about to send out another bill tomorrow morning. I assume you want me to send it?"

"Please do. And another thing. Send him a message from me. I want him in my office by next Friday, with that bill paid, or I'm gonna track him down with the police myself. You got that, Ron? Don't ever do a thing like this again. I hope we can take care of this without its causing any trouble."

"Me, too," Ron added sheepishly, as he slipped out of his seat and headed for the door.

The next Friday, Sylvia waited impatiently for Baka to make it to her office. She had just been told by the information desk that he had arrived for an appointment with her.

Baka entered her office the urban guerrilla she had met when he first came to visit Sara. Sylvia stared at him without speaking a word. Baka walked over to the large wicker chair with the bright red cushion.

Last Spring, he sank into that same crimson cushion and lost himself when he first met with Sylvia in her office. She continued to stare at Baka. She still said nothing to him.

"Ms. Sylvia," Baka offered, as sweetly as he could manage. The tone seemed to Sylvia so strange and somehow unconvincing, emanating from the image of pent up urban violence before her. With effort, she managed to suppress a smile, as she looked beneath the harsh veneer to the little boy under it.

"Don't be mad at me." Baka implored. "Trust me. I did nothin' wrong. I'm doin' nothin' you didn't do already."

"Baka," Sylvia said to emphasize her choice not to call him by his given name. "I want you to tell me right now what you are doing with the Hospital's access code, and where are you getting this money?"

"Ms. Sylvia," Baka repeated, tapping his well of self assurance, "I'm doing what I have to do. I left here last year with no place to go. I've made a place for me. For that, I have you to thank."

Sylvia didn't feel particularly good about that acknowledgment. At that moment, the image of godmother to the drug dealer just didn't seem appealing to her.

Baka continued, interrupting an awkward pause. "After leaving the Hospital, I stopped school and just started hanging around. I was out in the streets, where everything is possible and everything happens.

"I can't say that things were going real good when some downtown office-workin' junkie got in a bind with an acquaintance of mine in the supply field. He knew of some big deal that would make him the cash he needed to do more than get out of the bind, but he needed information. Then, I cut my deal.

"I asked him how much the information was worth, and how much he would pay me if I could get it. That downtown asshole . . . Oh! Sorry Ms. Sylvia, you know what I mean, . . . never thought I could ever do anything for him worth anythin', so he says -- thinkin' I'm some punk to play wit' -- that he'll pay me $10,000. I say deal and copped a phone number to reach the sucker.

"Then I called Ron . . . or Mr. Hammond to get access to the databases the Hospital used. We worked out our deal. I got the cash I needed from a street hustler friend, and I was in business. Now, I deal information.

"It seems I'm pretty good at it. There're always people who need somethin' that no one seems to want 'em to know. I find a way to get it. They pay me pretty good."

Sylvia continued to listen. She continued to stare at Baka. Still, she said nothing.

"Ms. Sylvia," Baka said, shifting in his chair to face Sylvia directly, "I'm not the little boy you dealt with last summer. I'm a businessman now.

"In the six months since I left this office, I've made $88,000 . . . in six months. That's just starting out.

"You want to take me to the police. Believe me, they will find nothin' to prove I did anythin'. You can't cut me off now that things are really flyin' for me. I need that access. But now, I can shop for the access I need and buy it anywhere. You know, I'd rather work out a more lucrative deal with you."

Baka said "lucrative" like a child playing with a new toy that his mother had just given him. Now, he stared at Sylvia.

Baka was playing the new game he had learned in his six months on his own. He was playing negotiator, the big deal maker. He was now starting to enjoy himself with his new adversary, Sylvia Forrest. He found the moment exhilarating. He imagined himself the lion tamer walking alone in the cage for the first time.

Only Baka did not realize that, in playing this game with Sylvia, he was truly playing out of his class. She was years beyond him in the daring he was just beginning to toy with. She had done this long ago, not as a game, but as life and death.

Sylvia stared back at him. Then, she just began to shake her head.

"Baka," she said, "you're still a little boy -- maybe a little boy with $88,000, but a little boy still. You're no businessman.

"Boy, a real businessman would eat you for lunch and have the leftovers the next day for breakfast. You don't know anything. You're just pressing your luck.

"What you're doing is illegal. The more you do it, the more likely you get caught -- or someone who has it against you informs. Then, what are you? Just another thug with a little money on his way to jail -- if you're lucky -- or maybe even dead. Is that what your grandmother would have wanted for you?

"I have little to say to you. Let's just say I can't say I'm disappointed in you, and I won't say I'm not. I can't accept that deal you offered. I can offer you one instead though."

" Baraka," for the first time Sylvia called him by his given name. "You think you're such hot stuff now. Well, I'll let you prove it by working for the Hospital. Not as an employee. God knows that you would not last long at the Hospital as an employee.

"Let's say we set you up in the information business and contract with you. We'll provide the access. We'll even provide the place. Now, before you get too excited, I'll tell you the quid pro quo. You know what that means, don't you, Baka?"

"Sure, Ms. Sylvia," he responded. "I'm a drop out. I'm not stupid."

"Well, Baka," Sylvia countered, "you aren't stupid, but you sure are ignorant -- even if you're in the information business. It's not that you don't know anything. You just don't know enough. You're too dumb for us to make money with. You have to change that. And that's the price.

"We're not investing in your unrefined ignorance. You've got to do something about that. Get schooling somewhere, somehow, but do it."

"O.K.," Baka accepted, "as long as I don't have to go to no punk school frontin' and kissin' someone's . . . ." Baka then caught himself and stopped immediately, adding, "You know what I mean."

"Baraka," Sylvia lectured now, "I may be the last person to know what you mean. It's only important that you know what you mean and that you know right now what I mean. Educate yourself or, Mr. Businessman, you're going to be hot only as somebody else's lunch."

Sylvia then asked, "Baka, tell me where you're keeping all that money you're telling me about? Is it in a bank? Are you investing it? Are you buying other businesses with it to make it grow? What is the big businessman doing to manage his business?"

Baka was challenged now. Only he did not know quite what to say that would impress Sylvia with his innate business acumen. "Well," he groped, "I still got it."

"How much do you still have, Baka?" Sylvia probed. "Where is it now?"

"It's where I can get my hands on it. That's all I need."

"How much has your money made for you sitting where you can get your hands on it?"

Finally, Baka had to give it up. "Ms. Sylvia, I know what you mean. I can't put all this cash no where without arousin' suspicion or gettin' the police interested in me. I'm into information, not laundry."

"Well, Baka," Sylvia opened, "it seems that the big businessman has a few things to learn. What you gonna do about it?"

"Why don't you just tell me what I'm gonna do, Ms. Sylvia? I get the idea that I'm gonna be doin' what you tell me anyway."

"Baraka," Sylvia said, staring at him with a sternness that, for a long time, no one had been interested enough to direct his way. "This is what you will have to do if this Hospital is ever again to do business with you.

"First, you'll accept the conditions of our business offer. We'll set you up in a place in the Village. We'll arrange for the computers and the access lines. You will have to manage your own access to the databases. We'll help you negotiate it. You'll have to hire your people, and manage your payroll, and keep your books, and take care of your own business planning.

"To make sure you can do all that, within 6 years, you get a college degree. Finish high school at night. Work out the GED. I don't care how you do it. Get in a college program. Learn the language. Learn the information that's out there that you say is your shop and trade. Learn how to run a business the right way before you decide to run it your way. Then, we'll really do business with you."

"Well, Ms. Sylvia," Baka conceded, "I can live with that."

"One thing more," Sylvia added, as Baka had just exhaled. "You know how we had this talk and how we had that talk last Spring that got you here in the Hospital? Well, you're gonna have these same talks now with the people you hire.

"Those people are going to be from the Village. I don't care if they are young. I don't care if they are in school or never finished school. You are going to hire them and make them as good at what they do as you think you are now.

"You are going to get them to find their way through school to find out what they don't know or what they know so well. In the end, you are not gonna let them go until they are better, stronger, and richer than you found them.

"You keep doin' that, you'll keep makin' us money. You keep makin' money for us, the more business we'll give to you. That's your debt, and it's my return on my *investment in you. I'm counting on you to keep me and mine well off."*

"Ms. Sylvia," Baka smiled, "That's extortion. You know that's illegal. Maybe, I should call the police on you."

"Well, Baka, more than anyone, you should know that there is a little outlaw in all of us. Just learn to make the outlaw work for you and not you for him."

"We gonna write this deal up, Ms. Sylvia?"

"You do the writing," Sylvia offered. "Send me a letter. I'll pass it to our lawyers. Do a good job and don't embarrass me. If you need any help, give Sara a call. She misses seeing you."

With that, Baka left Sylvia's office. Once again, Sylvia sat alone in her office, watching the bright day dissolve into dusk.

Learning Never Ends

In any healthy community, learning is life, and life is learning. Like any other living thing, a community that stops expanding what it knows looks a lot like an organism that has been dead for some time.

We take learning for granted. We like to think that learning is that noble enterprise that first occupied us at age five and ended with our walking across some stage to pick up a ribboned scroll. Yet, we do our greatest amount of learning before age five, and we reach our most profound insights after we have long crossed that stage in cap and gown.

For us to limit our attention arbitrarily to that time of life anywhere from ages five to twenty-five and to confine our vision within school house walls, we sentence ourselves to the fate of that dead organism. In short, we kill our community by limiting learning to school children and reserving its rewards only for them.

Ironically, to expand our vision of learning beyond our children, we propose that we focus upon our children -- not within the walls of our schools, but everywhere else in the community. We propose giving our children the lesson that learning is everywhere and goes on all the time, in order to teach that lesson best to ourselves.

The Community of Learning

In seeking to reestablish the importance of learning in our communities, we have proposed arraying the community's resources around learning. This focusing should occur on several levels. Physically, we have to identify and array facilities in our communities so that they support learning. These facilities include schools, but are not limited to them.

The objective is to reach our children where they are and move them to where they never had an idea they could go. To get to them, the community's facilities have to be where our children are. While our children are in the schools, they are also on the ball fields and playing courts, at the churches and mosques, at the malls, and on the streets.

The *community of learning* requires resources to do the things "ownership" contemplates. While such resources need not belong to the community, the community must ultimately direct their allocation and have those responsible be accountable to it for the resources and the outcome the resources produce.

The *community of learning* requires its own benchmarks. The community that benefits from this learning has needs and wants different from those of some other community. It requires its own benchmarks tied to its own definition of what success means.

The *community of learning* requires values. Learning requires discipline. Discipline assumes an acceptance of responsibility. Ownership conveys an understanding that we are ultimately accountable for the outcome of our learning system. In all of this, a *community of learning* embraces acceptance of values that do not arise spontaneously. We must be about changing how we think.

A Model of Community Learning

Imagine a community. It is now just as we see. On any given day, people mill about. The older men congregate on the street corners. The younger men pound a basketball at the base of a basketball hoop. The boys push and shove one another. The young women walk by, babies in tow. From time to time, someone rushes by, off to a job she more happily rushes from at the end of the day. Children come and go to schools they give no thought to when they leave and hardly much more when they return the next morning.

Life in many communities is full of empty spaces and empty time devoid of accomplishment. Many of us lack those chances to surprise ourselves about the possibilities our own efforts can make real. Many of us get too little opportunity to learn the most vital lesson: that learning makes us alive.

That lesson is one we do not need school to learn. For that lesson, we need just the chance to succeed at anything. With that lesson, we can then learn anything.

The *community of learning* is merely that community that has filled its empty spaces and empty time with opportunities for its people to accomplish things for themselves -- just to learn that they can.

In addition, the *community of learning* offers, in those empty spaces and that empty time, a chance for its members to pass on and share wisdom with one another. For this community, learning is its principal rite of passage.

The *community of learning* does not require gleaming schools and crisply new school book pages. It requires people committed to imparting to one another the knowledge to see others like them grow.

The model for such a *community of learning* provides a basis for understanding how the various elements of a community can come together. Most communities include an array of resources that support learning. Many of these resources we would hardly associate with schooling.

The resources in a community like Coppin Heights in Baltimore give an illustration of how just one community can take charge of its children's learning. That community contains potential partners from the academic world, business, religious, and other community institutions. These partners might include:

- Coppin State College
- Baltimore City Community College (Liberty Heights Campus)
- Frederick Douglass High School
- William H. Lemmel Middle School
- Baer Laboratory School (associated with Coppin)
- Various other public elementary schools
- Liberty Medical Center
- Various community congregations
- Mondawmin Shopping Mall
- Other community businesses
- Community social and civic groups.

All these partners are located within a short distance of one another in an area small enough to permit their cooperative interaction. In this collection of facilities, the community has at its direction varied resources and varied opportunities to reach its children. Working in partnership with its own institutions, the community can create for itself a structure that can provide

- instruction
- support and encouragement
- reward for achievement
- a shared new vision of what is possible for the community's children and also for the community itself.

171

By their interaction, these institutions can lead the people in the community to focus their priorities around filling its empty spaces and empty time with accomplishment, in particular, with the achievement of its children. Learning the joy of accomplishment is succeeding at making something that, but for your own effort, would not exist and securing due reward for your effort.

To support this education of achievement, the community must support the sustained effort necessary for accomplishment and assure that the effort sustained produces due recognition and reward. The role of the community's institutions is to provide the occasion for effort resulting in something palpable to be recognized and rewarded.

With the collection of academic facilities within the area, the community can address the needs of its children within a breadth of resources to develop the varied talents these children present. The community's vision of itself must be, however, broad enough to nourish the aspirations of those looking to pursue academics, together with those who would realize their potential developing in another direction, such as in business, or in service, or in the labor of their hands.

The collection of entities, particularly the business entities, represents monetary and other resources to make a *community of learning* possible. Money is just one resource needed. Political impact may direct other resources. Civic groups may leverage personal commitment to the development of children to spark achievement. Businesses may provide support and encouragement to parent employees to sustain a family commitment to learning.

172

Now imagine this transformed *community of learning*. Still, people mill about. The older men congregate on the street corners. They also spend their mornings with the younger men and older boys clearing and patrolling the marketplace that occupies the south parking lot of Mondawmin Mall. It began as a business venture with the students at Frederick Douglass High School.

The young men still shoot baskets into the twilight. However, the days of midnight basketball have yielded to night "net surfing" in the computer lab at Coppin State College.

People still rush off to jobs. Yet, they are in less a hurry to rush home. The time they spend after work is for themselves. They use the resources of civic and social organizations, and the community college -- off site -- to develop their job skills into a career or a home business.

Children still trudge off to school. Yet, they return to homes now in which they find adults engaged in the home work of learning what they do best. In time, these children will walk as adults across the stages of their lives to enter a new world.

In that new world, it is not just expected that they will some-how achieve and accomplish the things they choose to accom-plish. Here, their community takes for granted their accomplish-ment and just as routinely rewards it.

In the *community of learning*, learning occurs not just because we spend money to pay our teachers more than some other place, to build finer schools, or to provide better coaches for standardized testing. In the *community of learning*, learning occurs because it is made central to the life of the community and to the lives of those people who live there. Only the people in the community -- not the government or the well-intended people outside -- can make that community happen.

By taking stock of both its needs and its resources, people in a community can plan systematically to take charge of their own future. The community can seize control of its empty spaces and empty time where and when we otherwise say that it is all right for our neighbors and ourselves to do nothing.

To change the culture of our communities to be conducive to learning, we must first make the community confident about the value of its own accomplishment. Then, we must engage all of us in elevating the accomplishments each one of us shares with one another, by recognizing and rewarding such accomplishment as elevating *all* of us. The most effective targeting of such recognition and reward is to reach what we all care about most, however we may be situated -- our children.

The Benchmarks of Success for Learning in the Community

We look at our schools somehow as separate from our communities. It is as if, by some magic, there could be successful schools in failing communities. Perhaps, in the economy of public financing, it is easier -- and cheaper -- to think of fixing a school before making an entire community healthy. In the reality of the real world, such thinking is sheer fantasy.

A school that is apart from the community in which it is situated is simply irrelevant to anybody other than those whose pockets the school immediately serves. A dying community can only nurture a failing school. A school that produces successful graduates located in a dying community is of little use to that community.

From this standpoint, the conventional measures of school achievement that sever the success of the school from the health of its neighborhood may have little relevance for the people in the community. In that community, the only lesson that such schools teach with certainty is a bad one: that learning does not matter. The students such schools graduate earn a degree only in cynicism.

If the community is dying, the fact that its schools produce talented people means little. The students it produces obviously have little to do with the community or their talent does nothing for it. This appearance of success only begs what good the school might be.

Only the health of the community itself provides a suitable basis for defining, assessing, and establishing benchmarks and standards for learning having palpable meaning for the people in a given community. The community will have to establish for itself the measure of success that best makes sense for it.

We often speak of raising standardized test scores, or boosting SAT tallies, or increasing the number of students who advance from one grade to the next. What do these measures establish of use to people in the community? Unless the community can create some mechanism to take advantage of this achievement, the accomplishments of students do the community little good.

Worse, the benchmarks we select just focus our efforts in the schools on things that do not matter to the life of a community. Thus, a myopic focus on test scores or dropout rates may only result in cosmetic manipulation of the school population to maintain performance at, or even to surpass, a given standard.

For example, we say that standardized test scores should identify a good school. Yet, we nonetheless can reach our chosen benchmark, not by engaging students to pursue learning, but by eliminating those students who achieve poorly on testing. Such a measure may appear to speak well for what goes on inside the school. It does nothing about what is happening outside.

The issue here is not what should be the foolproof measure. Rather, the challenge for us is to state clearly to us what we want learning to do for our communities. Do we want learning just to increase the number of people who graduate from certain prestigious institutions of higher learning?

Or, is our focus more pragmatic? From the standpoint of the community, we may be looking for learning to elevate the conditions of life in the community. From this standpoint, the benchmark of successful learning in the community is not the progress of learning in the schools but the progress of the community.

Over a given period, has learning increased property values? Has it promoted more business opportunities or enhanced the public health of those living in the community? Or, has it elevated the quality of our lives in other ways to which we can readily point?

The people who help promote learning in a community demand different things of learning and the institutions we create to promote it. These people, the teachers and administrators of our schools, require proof *they* understand that shows they are doing their jobs. For *them*, these technical standards may have meaning.

However, those of us who live with the product of learning demand something else. We want a better life. Its measures we know without the technical assistance of experts or test scores. When we do well, learning does well. From this standpoint, we are the best measures and the best measurers in a community of how well learning goes.

Conclusion: *Who Owns the Community's Learning Institutions?*

Learning is the product of many things. It takes place in many locations other than the classroom. It happens at many times other than those framed by the school day.

Learning is a community resource. It binds the people who share the values, the background and the resources that identify community. It is therefore peculiar to ask who owns the community's learning institutions? Yet, it is necessary that we ask the question.

The simple answer is that we all do. Nonetheless, we act as though anyone else must: the teachers, the politicians, the federal government, the governor, this legislator or that administrator.

CLAIRVOYANCE

We wait for others to fix what is ours to make what we would have for ourselves. That no one but us can do.

We parent the children to be educated. We live in the communities whose futures will be shaped by what knowledge is imparted by and for us. We reap learning's rewards. We also bear the burden of its failure.

We must learn then how to act with the prerogatives of ownership -- not the halting and limited license that others might give us to speak. We are the community.

It owns its institutions of learning. It needs to take charge of them for itself. The fundamental question is not whether it has the authority to take charge of its own children's learning. The question is how ordinary people should do this. However, we will never know -- unless we try.

Connectedness
A Prescription for Living Well

We struggle day after day just to get by. We are aliens in a hostile world. As Africans exiled on North America in a world we did not shape, we share a common bond -- whether we are junkies looking for the next fix or investment bankers staking out the next deal. Our strange bond is our common isolation from one another.

In the distraction of surviving, we lose sight of the reality that we will always be the alien in this world -- until we make it our own by shaping it for ourselves. Yet, the demands of surviving keep us apart from one another and keep us away from our common need to remake the world to fit all the people like us.

If we are not whole, can we ever be well? We are disconnected from one another and from that world we would have for ourselves. Instead, we struggle to get by with something less than we want and maybe not much more than we need. We are too tired and too scared to let go of what little we have that does not serve us well to reach out for the more we can grasp to find satisfaction.

We speak of health care as if not feeling bad is doing well. Our thinking only underscores our dilemma. Do we truly believe that there is nothing more for us than just not feeling bad? What then do we do when what we do just not to feel bad keeps us from doing what makes us well?

We can therefore appreciate how the ease of the moment produces the pathologies of a lifetime for us. If I may never do well and can work only to get by, why not work myself to death just to have what little I can get -- or just do nothing at all? If my life will not amount to much anyway, what difference does it make if I abuse my body for a moment's pleasure or risk my life for the appearance of respect?

The cure our illness requires does not just address the pathology of our actions. It must root out the pathology of our thinking. The first step is to embrace the notion that just not feeling bad is not being well.

Survival is not health. Being alive is more than avoiding death. Our progress in North America must be more than the privilege not having to be society's Nigger. The structure that provides for our health must embrace these notions as well.

Thus, the issues of health care for African Americans cannot be the same as they are for the rest of the community. We are different. What may serve others well, need not serve us at all. If we are to be well, in a very fundamental sense, we must heal ourselves.

It is from this reality that we must approach health care policy. It is from this vantage that we must shape a policy that must not only make us healthy, but must make us whole and well.

Thinking About Our Health

What does it mean for me to be healthy? Start with asking me how I feel. Almost instinctively, I say "Fine. And you?" But does that mean that I am well -- or just too tired to involve you in the complications of my own life?

When we think about our health, we have a similar conversation with ourselves. Just as instinctively as we respond to the routine inquiry of strangers, we are as likely to respond to our own questions -- without much thought or perhaps without much hope.

On the one hand, I may casually tell myself that all is well. I have no pain or illness to think of that keeps me from going to work. I may not feel so good as I may once have felt. But, I tell myself, I am just getting old, or I wonder whether I feel any better or any worse than anyone else. In that concession to the misery around me, I conclude that there is some limited well of good fortune and good health reserved in the world for me. It seems that I am just getting my fair share -- even if it is not enough to make me well.

Or, on the other hand, I answer with the cold realization of how bad I may feel. I note that I have felt much better in the past. I hate what I do. The people I work with irritate me to no end. I have no peace in my home. I eat what always seems to disagree with my digestion. I see on television that I likely will die of some catastrophic condition. I see myself wasting away in some rest home my family cannot afford. Perhaps, I avoid that fate simply by being murdered on the streets. I conclude this cheery inventory of my condition with the happy thought that, even were I to mature to a venerable old age, there would be little to venerate about me. I might as well be dead, as quickly, or as painlessly, as I can manage. By the way, I may note with further ironic reflection, I am just fine.

There is yet a middle ground. I might approach the question this way: *For me to feel the way I want, what would it mean, what do I need, and can I find my way there?* If I can find my way to *feeling the way I want,* then truly I can respond, not that I am "Fine," but I can say that I am "well." At least, I can say that I will be "well." If I cannot even conceive of feeling good, can I ever say that I am "well" -- regardless the condition of my body?

When we think about health care as African Americans, we must first decide what we want. We might think about that inventory of ailments and pathologies that seem inevitably to confront us in our day-to-day living: cancer, AIDS, hypertension, diabetes, domestic violence, drug abuse, or early pregnancy complications. Or, perhaps, looking at them still, we might conclude that, if we can change the trend from more catastrophic to less, then we must be doing all right.

Even here, there is that troubling middle ground between just looking at the pathologies and looking cheerily to assess whether the cup is more "half full" than "half empty." We can assess not just how full our cup is, but what we want to be in it.

Health is more than not feeling bad. What then do we want that is, for us, *feeling good*? As we ponder feeling good, we may answer differently the question of what to do for the health of African Americans.

I focus on feeling good. Yet, I am then faced with the dilemma that the cost of relieving my suffering when I come to feel bad may prevent me from doing what I should have done to feel good in the first place.

Without even considering the technicalities of primary care, tertiary care, third party payer systems, HMOs, or the intricacies of actuarial tables that dominate present discussions of health care, we must get even more basic. What is our focus to be? Are we trying to enhance the ability of African Americans to reach current and future health care resources? Are we trying to redirect resources to deal more effectively with the ailments and conditions that plague Black folk?

Of course, these questions shape our inquiry on health care solutions that create a community in which African Americans can live well and prosper. Yet, the questions so framed assume other answers to other unstated questions. Our inquiry, therefore, must proceed from more basic questions leading to these more technical considerations.

What do we mean by Health? What must it include in a community in which Black folk get to feel good? What resources must be arrayed for Black folk to feel good? How must those resources be allocated, distributed and paid for to achieve the objective that African Americans feel good enough to enjoy living well?

Coming Home:
Finding the Way to Feeling Good

by
John H. Morris, Jr.

It should have been a happy day for Sara. She had worked hard to finish school and find a good job with an engineering firm that would have given her the chance to work on the kinds of projects that had filled her moments of intellectual fancy. She got the job a year ago.

Her mother could not have been more proud of her baby. She had all the opportunities that Sylvia lacked. Sara not only had completed her college degree, she had graduated from that fine New England engineering school where she had garnered honors now two springs ago.

Sara reflected on that cloudless May morning when all the sacrifice, worry, and hard work just dissolved in the fuzzy warmth of hugs from her mother and tears from her friends. She was so sure then that the world would just as warmly open up its arms to her and grant any demand she made of it.

On that fine morning, the air smelled of flowers. The ground was as soft as a cloud. The faces had nothing but smiles for her. Everything was possible.

Today was different. The October clouds would only darken her mood. Only now, Sara no longer had those moments of intellectual fancy. She only had questions about whether she had made the right decision for her life.

Sara stayed in bed much longer than her usual time. She looked around the bedroom of the condo she bought as a gift to herself and justified as her first investment with the bonus check she had received last Spring. It was a splendid view she had.

She looked out over the tree-covered hills, the leaves changing into spots of red and orange and yellow. They painted a stunning impressionist landscape against the coming grayness of a morning threatening rain. Under this cover of color, the landscape hid homes housing grim and dim lives of people maybe feeling as desperate as Sara did now.

Why had she left Du Bois Circle? Of course, she had to leave the home her mother had made to make her own place. But, why had she left Lexington Village? Surely, there was enough space there for her to find herself not so close to the shadow of her mother.

Then she remembered. She needed to be close to the offices she now dreaded waking up to go to. She would need the closeness of her new home to afford the freedom of staying late and coming in early to pursue the ambition of just doing the things she wanted to do with her work.

That was all a sad and cruel joke now. In the suburban offices of the area's largest building contractor,

Sara's ambitions just managed somehow to get lost amid assignments that meant nothing to her and the constant questioning of her promise.

After struggling with herself for another twenty minutes, she picked up the telephone. She dialed her number at work. When she reached her secretary, she muttered, in a voice masked with an affected hoarseness, that she was not well and would not be in the office that day.

She had done it. She had given in and given up. She would not go to work today for none but the simple reason she could not will herself to work. Sara was confused.

"What is wrong with me?" Sara grumbled to herself in exasperation. "I can walk. I can sit up. I can speak. So, why can't I work? Why do I feel so . . . I don't know what to call it? I don't feel outright bad. I can't say I feel all right. What's wrong with me?"

That afternoon, Sara met her mother at the Hospital for lunch.

Sylvia sat across from her 24-year-old daughter, not knowing what to say -- or even to think -- about her situation. All that she could manage to do was listen. Sylvia nodded empathetically more than once. She asked few questions.

What she really wanted to do was smack Sara and bring her back among the living. "What did you expect when you took that job? What made you think that you were so special that what had happened to so many before you would not happen to you?"

But Sara was Sylvia's baby, however much she may have needed a harsh dose of reality. Whatever medication Sara needed, Sylvia could not dispense it -- not on this day when her baby needed more from her mother than reality.

After both had finished the salads each of them had ordered, the conversation just seemed to wear down into a tense silence. Sylvia said nothing. Sara could not figure how to get out of her mother the magic answers to the questioning that left her immobile.

Sylvia broke the tension. "You gonna go to work tomorrow, baby? Maybe you can spend the day down here before you go back home tonight."

"Mama, I don't know what I'm going to do. I need some time away from work. Maybe, I will spend the day here in the Village. But, I got to get back to my own bed tonight."

"We can talk some more at dinner," Sylvia intoned, almost distracted by the passing of an older man in a dark suit. "Perhaps, by that time you will have thought through what you plan to do now. I've got a call I have to make, and you'd best get along with the rest of your day. You've got a lot of thinking to sort through, young woman."

For the first time, Sylvia was able to direct a smile at her now grown daughter that almost replaced the worry that had stamped her face all morning when she first heard from Sara. "Growing up's not easy, is it, honey?" She continued to manage a smile.

Sylvia moved to pick up her cafeteria tray and began her return to the myriad responsibilities that occupied her life now. She took a few steps and casually spun to face her daughter. "Have you seen Baka since you been down here? He always asks about you. It would be good to stop in on your old friend."

"I don't know, Mama. I don't know what I can say to Baka now. I'll think about it."

Sylvia said nothing further, but proceeded to take her tray to the return station. Sara remained seated alone at the cafeteria table, just staring at the glazed bottom of her salad dish still streaked with the tasteless concoction that passed for Italian dressing at the Hospital.

Before Sylvia disappeared to reenter the bowels of the Hospital, she took one last fleeting glance at her daughter. She found Sara lost in thought amid all sorts of heartache Sylvia had never known and could, in her mind, do little about. She turned and raced for her telephone, with the desperate hope that she had told Sara the right thing.

In the years that Vivien Thomas Memorial Hospital had been doing business with Baraka Bellamy, much had changed. With the help of Baraka's skill with information and the captive talent of the doctors and professionals who sought out the place, the Hospital had entered a variety of related fields.

To promote healthier lifestyles in the Village, the Hospital joint ventured with several local fitness freaks to open a health club. To relieve the pressure of crime around the Village, the Hospital established all sorts of treatment programs -- for drugs, violence, dispute resolution, and life counseling. It sought to deliver help and caring for the common complaints in the Village that affected the quality of people's lives.

At the center of all these ventures, there always managed to be BIA, Baraka Information Access, the corporation Baraka formed with the help of the Hospital to locate and assess information on-line. During this time, the 25-year-old Baraka had completed his degree requirements from the two local historically Black institutions of higher learning. He also had quietly acquired a nice sized investment portfolio for the day he hoped to bankroll the projects he chose to pursue.

It seemed, however, as though Baraka had been so occupied with the quickly developing events around him, that he had little time for a life of his own. He had not married or even given thought to a long-term relationship. After Sara went away to school, he somehow found little time that could not be used for any purpose unrelated to advancing his serious interests.

Sara found her way to the converted townhouse on Mitchell Terrace, just down the street from the old ele-

mentary school Sara had attended in simpler times. She knew the building well.

One of the really bad boys at the school had lived there with his family. She had endured his taunts and threats and sickening advances for a long time, until she managed to put him in his place by calling his bluff. She remembered watching his bully's bluster melt away into nothingness when she held her ground. Now, at this most vulnerable time for her, she had to return to his old house, just to please her mother.

She barely recognized the place. Surely, there was little about the Village that she could recognize from her youth. This place was no different. It was as though Baka had been a genie here who simply had waved a wand to transport this place somewhere out of her past memory to some enchanted land she yet could recognize. But, where was this place?

It hardly looked like the offices she was used to. It was neither downtown nor out in the Valley. She was hard pressed to put a word to it. For lack of a better description, it was home.

As profitable as she heard from her mother that Baka's operation had become, she was surprised by the informality of the place. No one wore a business suit. No one seemed to be dressed to make any particular statement other than the comfort of home. People openly walked around in their stockinged feet. She thought that a careful shoe thief might do well here.

Despite its informality, the place had its own stature. It had its own order. It had its own class. More than anything else, it had its own personality.

As Sara surveyed the scene, she was awakened by a cheerful "Hey sista, what can I do fo' ya? You lookin' fo' somebody?"

She turned to be startled by an arresting conflict of perception and reality. The obviously attractive young woman, who first appeared to her to be inattentive to her job, drawn to the latest soap opera in the middle of her work day, was in fact absorbed in a computer screen of text and numbers, working on something Sara could not even figure. She silently chastised herself for the too quick assessment. She told herself that she had been away from the Village far too long.

"Hey," the young woman uttered, looking up now to bring her attention fully upon Sara. "You all right, lady?" she pondered with a narrowing of her eyes.

"I'm just here to see Mr. Bellamy," Sara said in her most supercilious air, not wanting to let this young woman on to the fact that she and Baka were old friends. For some reason, the presence of familiarity in this workplace made Sara uneasy. She needed the distance of social formality. Or, so she thought, not wanting to show any of her present desperation to people she hardly knew.

The young woman was puzzled. She repeated out loud, "Mr. Bellamy? . . . You sure he work here?"

Then, in an instant of recognition, her puzzlement dissolved into a warm smile that opened up the brightness of her face. "Oh, you mean, Baka. Why didn't you just say that in the first place? Just go on up the stairs to the long hall way. Just call for him. He'll be out."

Sara pointed hesitantly to the staircase that led to the second floor, both inquiring about the way and asking permission to go up. She got no response from the young woman, who had simply assumed that Sara would go immediately. The young woman was again absorbed in the flashing images before her.

As Sara arrived on the second floor, she caught a glimpse of something approaching her that she wanted to call Baka. But, she wasn't sure that this thing was real. The one clear point of identification was the shaven head. Everything else was foreign.

Sara would have recognized a more mature version of the urban guerilla she once knew. But she did not find the old fatigue pants, the combat boots, flack jacket and goggle sunglasses. She encountered now the urban prophet, fully clad in sandals, a long patterned robe-like-thing over a pair of jeans, and a small pair of wire glasses, untinted, balanced delicately on a face the bottom half of which was now obscured by a full beard.

"Baka?!!" Sara said, her eyes narrowing then opening wide with recognition. Before he could acknowledge her greeting, decorum left her.

Sara ran down the hall way and just enveloped Baka in her long arms. Baka remained the fireplug he had always been. As she brought his humanity close to hers, Sara now towered over Baka.

At that moment, more than she had ever felt in her life, she wanted to cry. Still, she fought to keep her composure.

"Sara," Baka smiled, as he pushed her back to arms' length to get a fuller view of her. "How you doin'?"

"Oh, I'm O.K., I guess," she quickly muttered, as he offered to show her around BIA.

To the surprise even of this expertly trained engineer, she found more space used creatively in this town house than she could have imagined in her wildest intellectual fancies at college. In this room and that one, Sara found a place where work joined seamlessly with life.

Last, she came to Baka's space. She hardly could call it an office. That would have been an insult to the spirit of the place. To call this space an office would have been to call a busy family kitchen a tomb. Even empty, without a soul in sight, this space was teeming with life and personality. As she surveyed the scene, the engineer marveled at how well the space said but one thing -- Baka. It was just an extension of him.

In looking at the room, Sara saw much that she never knew about her old friend, the urban guerilla. She saw books. There were neatly shelved volumes and a few disarrayed stacks.

CLAIRVOYANCE

The room was commanded by a large table. On close inspection, Sara saw that this dominating presence was just a very well worked piece of wood on two saw horses. She found a closet that passed for a pantry, with all sorts of canisters of crackers, pretzels, nuts, and dried fruit. In one corner of the room, she scanned a small refrigerator, with empty bottles of fruit juice on top. Distributed at random throughout the room were soft comfortable chairs and pillows on the floor. Unifying the disparate elements of this special space was a thick, warm rug, woven of a soft pile in colors that reminded her of the southwest.

The only concession to work in this space was the personal computer, monitor, keyboard and pointer positioned on the corner of the table. It was a space in whose apparent chaos, she could see only order. In the informality of its order, Sara saw only comfort.

She was immediately at ease in this place. She let herself sink deep in the brightly colored chair to the right of the table. Baka descended to rest in the lounging chair just on the other side of the table. He yawned, lifted his sandal clad feet, and stretched out lazily the short length of his body.

Sara and Baka spent the next hour or more together, recounting old times, new times, family and friends. For the entire time, Sara said nothing about what had brought her in town to have lunch with her mother.

It was Baka who forced the issue. "Sara, what's wrong?"

"Baka, what makes you think that something's wrong?" Sara attempted to fend off the inquiry. "Why do you want to spoil the moment, Baka, by insisting that we talk about me?"

"Sara, your mother thinks that somethin's wrong, and she wants me to talk with you about it. So, let's get on with it. Talk to me."

"Baka, it's just not that easy. I'm not a database. I don't know what you want from me. I just don't feel right."

Baka probed, "You just don't feel right about what, Sara?"

"If I knew that, do you think I would be down here in the Village all day?" Sara offered, growing increasingly irritated with Baka's questioning about this very sore issue.

But Baka felt her tenderness about this subject and just refused to let up on his old friend. "Why did you come back to the Village today?

"Look, Sara," Baka rejoined, "You leave school, go off to college in Boston, come back to town, move out to Hunt Valley, and it's been years since I've seen you. Suddenly you're back in the Village. If nothin's wrong, then somethin's goin' on. What's up then, Sara?"

Sara continued to struggle. She struggled against Baka's curiosity. She struggled to maintain the composure she valued as her greatest asset. She struggled to find the words to convey her pain. Still, she could do little but avoid his glare. She could do little to escape his many questions.

Her only response was to mutter, "Baka, I can't say. You just wouldn't understand. I just don't feel good anymore about anything."

Then there was silence. Baka stopped asking questions. Sara embraced the relief silence brought and just slumped down in the large soft chair to the right of Baka's desk.

Baka waited, and waited, and waited some more, as if he expected something miraculous to happen. Nothing did.

"Sara," Baka muttered softly, "I can't feel your pain, and I'd be the last to presume to tell you how you feel. Now having said that, I'm gonna be fool enough to try.

"Maybe, it might help you to consider what I think I see when I look at you," Baka began. "I see a pretty little girl who sees herself this bad Black woman who took on Boston and won honors. She thinks she can be all that anytime she wants. Now, she's playing with the boys in Hunt Valley, and they don't want to play with her, much less let her win anything. Dealin' with the White folks can be real rough.

"Bet you never gave it a thought when you took that offer they made you with stars in your eyes. Maybe, you thought they'd let you win because you're smart or pretty or worked hard. Didn't you know it doesn't matter, Sara?

Nobody like us is supposed to win with them -- unless they say so. I don't think you want to win like that, do you?"

"Baka," Sara said haltingly, "I don't know what you're talking about. Remember, I lived here. I don't see me running away the way you seem to think. I just want to do the things I dream seeing myself doing. I just saw that happening with the firm. Now, I just am uncertain about everything -- especially me.

"Everything feels bad. My back. My head. My life. All right, Dr. Baka, if you know so much, what do I do?"

"Girl, that's real simple. I suppose somebody might say that you're young, and you should be patient. That ain't where I'm at. I can give you my prescription in just two words: Come home."

Sara turned and stared at Baka. "Come back to the Village?! Run away from Hunt Valley and come back to the Village with my tail 'tween my legs?! I'd thought you'd be the last person to say that, Baka."

"I didn't say that, Sara. I just said 'Come home.' You figure out what that means for you. Maybe, it's gettin' out of Hunt Valley. Maybe it's going back and kickin' ass. I can't tell you, Sara. You got to tell you.

"It clearly is you takin' care of you -- not you takin' yourself on. Give yourself a break. Find out what you deserve to do for you -- and then get it done."

"Yeah, Baka," Sara said, as her voice trailed off to another thought. *"What are you talking about? And what does it have to do with me?"*

"What makes you think you so special, Sara?" Baka asked with an unintended challenge. Before Sara could hurl back a response to this invitation to strike back, Baka clarified, *"Do you think that you're the only person who feels the way you feel?"*

"Well, Baka," Sara responded, *"I'm the only one inside my skin experiencing the stuff I have to endure who has to do anything about it."*

"That's not what I mean," soothed Baka, trying to make up for any affront to an old friend. *"Maybe, you're not alone in going through this. Maybe, you can talk to others having the same trouble. I don't know. It might help."*

"O.K. Baka," Sara conceded. *"I hear you. But why should I think that you're in such great shape? What do you do that makes you think you're so special not to hurt?"*

"Sara," chuckled Baka, *"how do you know I don't?"*

Sara smiled and felt a joy she had not known for a long time. Then, she remembered the friendship they had treasured so long ago. She comforted in something she had long forgotten and missed -- true friendship and personal intimacy.

They talked into the early evening -- and after dinner at Sylvia's dining room table. Before it was too late, Sara *excused herself and drove home. So the evening ended. So the idea began.*

Once she had seen beyond herself, the thought occurred to Sara that others out there needed to learn how to come home. Home was safe. Home was health. Home was where we could be comfortable enough to let ourselves feel good.

That was the idea. Call it a strategy. Call it a plan. As she talked with Baka, they hatched the notion that health for people like them meant more than an inventory of working body parts. She took Baka's advice 'to find out what you deserve for yourself and get it done.' She thought about how to package an array of opportunities for people like her looking to find the life they deserved to make for themselves.

At home, she sat at her computer terminal -- always her mother's daughter. She just listed the things she wanted to feel good. She began: Eating well, exercise, regular medical care, spiritual development, and she went on. As she compiled her list, she added something so simple she had forgotten it entirely -- friendship.

The October night carried the sharp edge of coming winter. The chilled air made Sara sleepy at last. This time, she sensed that sleep would also bring rest. But before she squeezed herself between the sheets, she had one more task to perform.

She called up another document on her computer screen. She then began:

Dear Mr. Flanagan:

I hereby resign. I am going home.

That was enough. She saved the document. Sara turned off her computer screen, then her lights. She climbed into her bed. In the warmth of her approaching challenge, she drifted off to a restful sleep.

The Challenge of a Healthy Future for Black Folk: *Empowering the Powerless to Heal Themselves*

Our current thinking about health care only celebrates our impotence. It opens its arms to the helpless. It embraces the hopeless. Despite its good will and its good work, after it has relieved our infirmities, it leaves those of us it nurtures infirm in our dependence upon it.

For African Americans, that dependence is as much an infirmity as any ailment our medicine now treats. Perhaps, that dependence is especially fatal to us because dependence has been the narcotic we have long been given to cure our many ills or just to still our shrill and hoarse cries for relief.

That cure has sustained us, trapped in the infirmity it nurtures. For us, dependence is a hard habit to kick. Yet, we will not be well as a people until we are dependence free.

The challenge of a health care solution for African Americans that works for African Americans is to heal without dependence.

A solution that instills dependence, while it purports to heal, may only relieve suffering. It will not make Black folk well.

The puzzle of a dependence free health care model poses a fundamental enigma: you cannot heal me without making me dependent upon you -- at least for my healing. The only healing solution, however, that leaves me dependence free is one that allows me to heal myself -- without you.

So we pose our health care challenge in simple terms: to heal African Americans, the cure must leave us independent as well. This challenge dictates several policy requirements that vary significantly from many models currently proposed. In addition, the requirements also raise other issues that confront us with fundamental choices in values.

Health care solutions supporting the independence of Black folk will compel the following policy shifts:

- Refocusing health care resources from treating and relieving suffering to preventing the ailment that caused it
- Rethinking the financing structure to support a disease-prevention-based model
- Reshaping our notions of compassion to view differently both present day choices to live a life of excess and waste that lead to future suffering and the present day suffering resulting from the past unwise decisions that people freely made for themselves
- Accepting a structure created by, maintained by, and benefitting principally the health care and other interests of African Americans

- Recognizing that African American "ownership" of the health care structure is a health issue, not just a matter of fairness or economics.

Making Community a Home for Feeling Good

The focus of this health care vision for African Americans is community. In community, we possess the assets to assert ownership: the understanding of our own value and a framework for acting upon that value to secure our own worth.

We have access to the structures to control the health care options available to us. We also have the culture to support the understanding that transforms the goal of health from relieving suffering to assuring wellness. Most significantly, in community, there is the basis for reconnecting Black folk with one another to make us whole again.

Consider a community like the fictional Lexington Village of these continuing vignettes. It is a community populated almost exclusively by African Americans. It has created for itself an economy that works for African Americans. It has demonstrated the value to Black folk of sharing a common vision of our own prosperity. It has created a world in which African Americans are at the center. Finally, it has also created for itself values and structures that embody those values that allow for cooperative action.

Within that community are numerous institutions that reach the members of that community every day to support the community's activity and values. Those institutions within which the community reposes trust include its places of worship, its schools, its businesses, its social and fraternal groups, and also its civic, charitable and political organizations.

What do these community institutions say and do about the health of the community and its members? They could organize to advocate for the community to others whose control of health care resources they thereby acknowledge. In such advocacy and in such organizing, these institutions may also concede their own impotence. The health care they so secure also underscores the impotence and dependence of the people in the community.

What then would a community of empowered people do? In a place like Lexington Village, with people like Sylvia Forrest and Baraka Bellamy, the community would seize the initiative and recognize its own basis for power. That power may not be the power of protest. Rather, it may be the community's present ability to disrupt and devastate the present system and to save it as well.

The people in such a community would make the following observations:

- Few people, by themselves, no matter how well off they may be financially, pay for the health care they receive.
- The financial stability of the health care system depends upon the correctness of the actuarial assumptions of insurance companies or governments.
- Under the assumptions of the present system, Black folk are generally viewed as financial risks to the system, as

long as the system is expected to render care meeting the needs of African Americans.

- Those in charge of the present system avoid catastrophe in dealing with Black folk by providing us the appearance of coverage and avoiding the reality of service.

The members of such an empowered community would not accept these observations as immutable truths. Rather, they would use them strategically to attack the present system and to establish one of their own.

They would recognize that those now in control of necessary health care resources are limited by their own assumptions about things of which they have little understanding or control. These empowered people would then use their better grasp of these things and greater control of them to leverage the resources of others to satisfy their own interests.

For example, the present system identifies the health care needs of African Americans as reflecting actuarial assumptions like the following:

- Black folk are more prone to violence and require care to address trauma, rehabilitative services, or prosthetic equipment.
- The stresses on African Americans create certain other stress-related ailments, resulting in needs for treatment of domestic violence, drug dependency or mental health conditions.
- The diet of African Americans, the stresses of our lives, or other hereditary considerations may produce the need

204

for treatment of hypertension, diabetes, heart disease or cancer.

From these assumptions predicting future health care needs of African Americans, those who make money providing care can better arrange their resources in the way that assures them the greatest profit. Health care providers can plan accordingly to have their resources ready to deal with these future needs. Insurers also can plan accordingly to avoid future claims.

With its financing ultimately tied to insurance, the financial health of the health care system depends upon the accuracy of its actuarial assumptions. The system therefore can be controlled by whoever can change the behavior underlying those assumptions. With such change, the system becomes economically blind.

Whoever can function as health care's "seeing-eye dog" wields substantial power. Accordingly, those empowered people in this community will seize control of their own health care options by making the system blind and then controlling its ability to see -- at least regarding Black folk.

Within an empowered community, it is therefore possible for people to do the following things:

- To act in their own interests to change what they do
- To state their own interests by setting their own agenda
- To determine the value of what they do to extract their worth from others for themselves.

Under this approach, consider the following tableau in Lexington Village. The Village's institutions have organized themselves to promote health. They have established a regimen of what is good to eat and what is good to do to make the body stronger and more impervious to infirmity. They have created approaches to reducing violence, encouraging pregnancies later in life where there are fewer complications. They work to offer better prenatal and post natal care, together with family support and development. The Village has created opportunities for health education, health counseling, supervised exercise, and new options for healthful eating.

The Village has taken action not just out of a belief that good health is its own reward. Rather, it has its own actuarial assumptions that project the value of its changed behavior to those in charge of health care resources. It is looking to leverage that value into monetary reward to all the members of the Village who, by their changed behavior, contribute to realizing that value.

In addition, the empowered community would set the agenda to support its ability to maintain its changed behavior and the financial return that it achieves from that change. It would secure with its enhanced participation in the health care system, a greater and more lucrative role for people who, like themselves, better understand the assumptions underlying their interests.

The empowered community would promote the expansion of opportunities for actuaries who look like themselves, together with the underwriters, the professionals, the other people who also support the new preventive activities of education. This expansion of these opportunities creates economic opportunity for people like themselves to deal more profitably with other people like themselves.

In the end, the system succeeds in making the people in this community well in every sense. It creates an economic environment that supports their dreams to do as they would choose for themselves. It provides the opportunity for them to control and avoid the infirmity that would make them dependent upon others. It provides the basis for treatment by others like themselves, without having to accept wellness under conditions that may diminish who they are. Finally, it sustains them in their connectedness with one another. In this sense, it creates for the people in our empowered community, wherever we may be, a home that will always nurture and sustain us as who we are.

Moving Toward Prevention

We cannot all be doctors. We cannot all be nurses. We cannot all become lay practitioners of medicine treating our own ailments. Thus, once we become ill, we therefore become inevitably dependent upon the skill, training, and expertise of someone other than ourselves.

If we are then striving for health care solutions that preserve and support our independence, it is apparent that the focus of our health care solution must be on keeping us from getting sick in the first place. That focus then must be on prevention -- to assure our own independence and autonomy.

We cannot perform open heart surgery on ourselves to ease the pain of angina from acute coronary disease. However, we can inform ourselves of the risk elements. We can control what we choose to eat. We can exercise to reduce the risk of disease. We can make the choices in lifestyle to combat the harmful effects of stress. We can do any number of things to treat the coronary disease, before it becomes acute, that avoid the need for subjecting ourselves to dependence upon the skill and monitoring of someone other than ourselves. Thus, dependence is not a necessary element of health care.

The focus of a prevention-based model is different from that of a treatment-based model. Under the treatment approach, resources are directed to relieving suffering through access to professionals whose job it is to restore health to people in poor health. In contrast, the resources of a prevention model are aimed at maintaining already healthy people in such a state of health as to reduce the suffering within a population by avoiding it altogether.

The resources in a treatment-based system are ideally focused on a presumably small population of unhealthy people, suffering some condition that requires treatment. We use that framework when we are sick, and the framework ideally responds to our need. The resources of a prevention-based model are ideally allocated to as broad a population of healthy people, seeking to maintain a present state of good health.

Obviously, these two different frameworks strive to do different things. Just as obviously, they have common elements. Certainly, a treatment-based model is not indifferent to prevention, and a prevention-based model cannot be indifferent to human suffering. These fundamental distinctions do not reflect differences of purpose, but differences of focus. In this regard, the approaches require different structures, different kinds of professional staffing, different resources, and different kinds of support.

Financing Prevention

In a prevention-based system, we invest in the good health of the client population to avoid the cost of illness and reap the financial reward of wellness. The economics of our present framework is a little different and a little more complicated.

There are several economic frameworks. For example, there are the economics of the health care providers, the economics of the insurers or underwriters, and the economics of the suppliers of the providers, *i.e.,* the people who make treatment equipment and pharmaceuticals.

Doctors, nurses, administrators, and other health care professionals make money from providing care for a fee paid by, or for, people in need of their services. Generally speaking, people do not seek out the services of these professionals unless they are suffering to such an extent that expense is not a factor or someone pays for them to see a professional.

The professionals in this system depend financially, therefore, upon people who are sick, or who are seeking to avoid being sick, or who have the means to pay whether or not they are sick. If there are more people who are sick than have the means to pay, or if there are few people who are sick, whether or not they can pay, the health care professionals will have trouble making money.

Most health care costs are paid by insurers. These insurers are either private companies or governmental insurers. Private companies make money gambling that they will take in more money in premiums and in the investments they make with the premiums than they will have to pay out in health claims. Government simply seeks to maintain a desired level of health in the community for the tax dollars it commits to pay to care for those it deems to help.

Whether private or not, insurers depend upon the productivity of the healthy to pay for the sick. If they gamble wrong about how sick people may become, or if more people are sick than they plan for, or if the healthy are less productive and therefore less able to pay, the private insurers lose money and governments break budgets.

The suppliers of the health care professionals, the medical equipment people and the drug manufacturers, also depend, if not on the poor health of folks, at least on our concern not to be sick. These professionals require people, whether sick or not, in need of diagnosis or treatment. As with the health professionals, if there are a lot of people who are sick and who do not have the means to pay, or, if there are few people who are sick, whether or not they can pay, then these people have trouble making money.

The financing of our present scheme benefits generally from the poor health of at least some of us. While the professionals who treat us may be concerned with relieving our suffering, their livelihoods are largely dependent upon that suffering.

Insurers, on the other hand, have every incentive to promote the health of all of us to defray their risk in underwriting the care for our illness. However, they have chosen generally to limit their risk, not by investing in the healthfulness of all of us, but in finding ways to underwrite only the healthiest of us.

The combination of these financial consequences portends only financial catastrophe for the system or a health care disaster for African Americans. The focus of the health care professionals has been to increase our ability to detect, identify and treat sickness. We have done so at escalating cost. The import of our cost underwriting practices has been to limit underwriting either to those most able to pay or those least in need of paying because they are in good health already.

If these underwriters should see African Americans only as the objects of pathology, with little real productive potential, they then have no financial incentive to view us as the subjects of underwriting. As the health professionals enable us to focus more on what makes us sick, the attention of the underwriters directs us more away from the treatment to relieve our distress. Accordingly, the structure of present financing gives us the itch but may deprive us of the wherewithal to scratch. On the other hand, the cost of our scratching to our satisfaction may just bankrupt this system -- as it is now configured.

The alternative we propose is a different model altogether. Our solution matches the health options with the financial incentives of underwriters to make feasible the idea of broad coverage for everyone, without the specter of financial collapse. The only model that offers such a prospect is a prevention model.

A prevention model does not require a different financing structure. It merely involves differing financing assumptions. In addition, we must recognize that, in financing prevention, we are not financing treatment, but behavior modification. This change in focus dictates a different allocation of resources from care taking to behavior incentives, information and support.

The principal assumption of the prevention model is that sickness is often the result of behavior choices. Change the choices people make, you decrease how often they get sick and the severity of the sickness. With that reduction, you should get two financial benefits: (1) care is less costly; and (2) the people are more healthy and, *with access to the productivity of the economy*, more able to sustain the cost of prevention and the reduced treatment required.

A prevention model permits a reduced allocation of resources to treatment and an expanded allocation to modifying behavior from costly to productive conduct. By modifying the behavior of the would-be patients under the treatment model, health care resources under the prevention approach can be directed to support, *at the same time*, both the physical and the fiscal well-being of the people to be served.

In this way, the health care and the financial objectives of the system are not in conflict. The system does not then have to choose between the health of the people it would serve and its own solvency. Its solvency then depends directly and necessarily upon the health of its clients.

Under this prevention model, it is then possible to conceive realistically a framework in which African Americans can be well, without requiring the kind of assistance that may also instill a disabling dependence. More directly, it is feasible to think of a framework that provides for the health of people and also their independence.

The Values of Prevention

In a health care framework that is dependence free, the focus on prevention must permeate the culture of the people providing health care services and those receiving them. For us now, compassion for those who suffer is not just a motive for granting access to care, it is virtue. It carries with it other values and compels other choices in how we frame the fundamental questions of our lives.

Within the treatment model, personal autonomy is an assumed value. Individual compassion is the controlling concern. We treat suffering because we value the virtues of the Good Samaritan.

You value your compassion toward me, even to the extent it undermines my autonomy. For example, you provide me care, in your compassion, even when I do not want to be cared for. The care your compassion affords may just affront my dignity. Your compassion, however, insists that my life continue, even if the treatment that keeps me alive may not make my life worth living to me.

Still, within the limits of your compassion, you purport to recognize my autonomy. You tell me that I can express my autonomy in your preference that I choose my care provider -- as long as I can afford to pay for the care. If I cannot pay for the care, your compassion still affords me care, but without the prerogative of choice. Or, should I seek to end the indignity of your treatment of me, my condition must be so dire as to be beyond the assistance of your compassion.

213

The point of this discussion is not to dismiss the compassion of the treatment model but to emphasize its priority of values and better understand the consequence of its view of prevention. The compassion of the treatment model arises from the relationship of the care giver and the care receiver.

In a treatment model, the interests of the care giver control. That is not to say that those interests are selfish or not truly compassionate. It is only to point out that its view of compassion is from the vantage of the care giver. That point of view is not necessarily that of the person in need, but of the person who must witness the need and may want, for his own reasons, to do something about it. The focus of the provider becomes that of making the effort, not necessarily upon achieving a response satisfactory to the one in need.

The values of compassion do not resolve the dilemmas of care. Rather, these values merely help define what dilemmas arise from the provision of care. Within this model, the moral dilemmas of care are generally a variation of this question: "What are the limits of my compassion?"

We have seen these dilemmas played out especially where the treatment we would provide to prolong life merely prolongs suffering. Similar issues arise when the extraordinary suffering we can see, but do little about, so commands every extent of our ability even to respond to other suffering just beyond our view.

In dealing with this latter dilemma, we do not directly choose who to let suffer. We do not consult the suffering to help us decide who to help. We just close our eyes and address the pain closest to us and force our own satisfaction with that solution.

The prevention model requires its own array of values and priorities. With prevention, compassion is an assumed virtue, and autonomy is the controlling value. We support prevention because it empowers people to control their own lives. We accept the value of autonomy because we seek the benefit that flows from people acting empowered.

You respect my autonomy. In my autonomy, I chose poorly and suffer greatly because of my choice. Within a prevention framework, the dilemma we face is how can you relieve my suffering and still respect the autonomy of the choice that led to my suffering. Or stated differently, how can I accept your comfort without denying my independence? Your comfort also relieves me of the consequences of my choosing that makes me independent.

Within the treatment model, the dilemma is resolved by diminishing the chooser and the choice. We say that the chooser cannot be held accountable for his choice, since we have the power to relieve his suffering. Accordingly, within the treatment framework, we reward bad choices and disregard those people who choose wisely.

We cannot afford such generosity under a prevention framework. There, we must reward the wise chooser and allow those who choose poorly the unhappy consequence of their unwise choices. Otherwise, how else do they learn to choose better? Where then is our compassion, if we do not allow the lesson to play itself out?

Ignoring the compassion embodied in letting me alone to learn to choose better, the only compassionate alternative then is for you to take care of me. The challenge in a prevention model is not to find the resources that allow you to take care of me, but to find the compassion in supporting me to take care of myself.

Under the prevention model, compassion is respecting autonomy and educating, encouraging and supporting others to choose wisely for themselves. It cannot be exercising the choice for them that avoids suffering.

The prevention model assumes the value of independence. We also have to embrace that assumption in how we view ourselves and others. That understanding requires an underlying faith in, and respect for, the ability of others to choose correctly for themselves. Thus, we necessarily must respect the choice of others no matter how uncomfortable the outcome may make us.

In proceeding with a prevention model, we must accordingly confront new ethical dilemmas in providing care. We cannot resolve these dilemmas from the assumptions of a treatment approach. We must therefore fully explore and understand the assumptions and values of prevention.

The Prerogatives of Ownership

The challenge for any model of health care that works for Black folk is managing to assure care without also creating dependence and thereby relieving people of responsibility for themselves. The particular challenge of a prevention model is how to provide treatment without undermining personal autonomy.

These dilemmas are avoided with an appreciation of ownership. It is one thing to be cared for by a stranger you may view as different and superior, who provides care through means that are not yours. It is another thing to be cared for by someone who is like you and more a peer to you. It is still another thing to be cared for by someone who is a peer and whom you accept as clearly working *for* you.

The context in which treatment is given can determine the extent that caring for means taking care of. The issue raised here is the need to care for people without taking care of them. We now accept care in contexts in which we relinquish autonomy and in which deference is expected.

When we consider treatment options for African Americans, we often do so without considering the prerogatives of ownership. We assume instead all the earmarks of deference. We assume that treatment is the prerogative of the good people who provided the care. We assume that those good people are other than the African Americans who secured the treatment.

With the care, we do not also assume ownership. Ownership changes the relationships of the people within any health care system in one important way. Without ownership, the people receiving care in the system are merely the objects of the good will of the care giver. With ownership, the care giver is merely the instrumentality by which the owners secure their own well-being. In this important respect, ownership becomes a necessary element of any system that respects the independence of the people *receiving* care.

CLAIRVOYANCE

We can express ownership in several ways. We can own in real financial terms. We can own in the sense that we control the system's outcomes. We can own to the extent that the assumptions of the system are our assumptions. We can own when the values the system embodies are our values.

What is our status in any system when someone else has a financial stake in the outcome of health care decisions involving our health? What independence do we have when someone else dictates the health outcomes available for us? What respect can we enjoy from a system that makes unstated assumptions for us, and about us, on things we would find insulting if stated to us directly? What good is any good will to me if I do not ever get to choose what good means?

The ultimate question ownership poses is whether the system exists for us or do we exist for the system? The simple answer is that any system exists for whomever owns it.

How can we own the system financially when no one person or group of people can write a check large enough to challenge any of the financial entities now intimately involved in the health care system? As with anything else involving the condition of Black folk, this question of finance involves merely recognizing and understanding our financial value within the current system better than anyone else.

In a system funded ultimately by insurance, that value is tied to our ability to avoid an insurance loss. Within the health care system, that loss arises from a claim for treatment that cannot be paid from existing premiums. For example, people may have paid sufficiently into the system to be entitled to treatment. They now seek access to the system with an illness requiring treatment costing far more than any one person has ever paid.

We add value to the system to the extent that we provide an abundance of premiums paid into the system over a shrinking pool of claims made against it. For example, we assure behavior resulting in a measurable increase by us in productive activity increasing the premiums received from us. At the same time, we measure a decrease in claims made by us that the system otherwise would have to pay.

We thus have defined the economic value of our wellness to the system such that we could demand a return for our efforts. The only issue would be developing the structure that allows for such value to be created, measured, and bargained for.

With a basis for securing return for our own health care decisions, we then make those health care decisions for ourselves. We receive for those decisions not just good health from someone else's efforts. We receive financial reward from our own effort.

From that effort, those who would otherwise be our care givers become our trading partners. The people who once provided care out of their good will now provide it because of our financial interest.

In this sense, we benefit from a health care system that strengthens us financially, requires our productivity, and deals with us to preserve that productivity. For their own self-interest, these care givers require our good will rather than insist that we defer to their good will.

Control, as ownership, is merely figuring out how to exercise the power to have the system satisfy the interests we define. As with many other things involving our exercise of power, our power may not reflect the capability that any one of us individually may have, but our ingenuity in harnessing the power that all of us possess *together*.

Health care's reliance upon insurance offers to Black folk both the structure and the opportunity to take advantage of our numbers. No one person pays for health care. With our health insurance premiums, we all share the payment obligation. With the choice we make in selecting an insurer, we can influence a range of health care decisions.

For example, we respond better to people like us. If we have the ingenuity to organize our own decisions about the particular insurer we select, we can direct our insurer to demand the kind of care givers who serve our interests.

It may be that workplace stress particularly afflicts us. Yet, the menu of treatment options available does us little good. By finding strategies and structures that make resources more responsive to our insurance dollars and the return on our productivity to underwrite our care even more, we can compel financially a different allocation of resources. We can focus these resources more on relieving the stress that may plague us especially.

By establishing our value as health care participants who can generate premiums and reduce costs, we can also change the assumptions that shape our health care options. It may be said that the present system makes the following assumptions about us that diminish both our value and autonomy:

- Our participation in a health care system can only mean substantial expense.
- As recipients of care, we need others to show us what is in our own interests.
- We bring nothing of value to the health care system other than our need.
- As participants in this system, our role is limited to that of subjects in need of care.
- As participants in this health care system, we are nothing more than the embodiment of the pathologies others see in us.
- We represent a challenge to the system to save costs by reducing coverage.
- As recipients of care, we deserve only the care we happen to receive.

These assumptions shape how the current system responds to us. Seeing us only as a potential and substantial economic drain, current practices premise their economic survival on strategies to reduce -- not expand -- coverage for those of us who look least like those in charge of the system. To the extent that coverage is desired, it is desired under an economics that allows for coverage and payment without necessarily requiring care.

Having no understanding of our value, those in charge often accord us no value at all. The result is widespread arrogance toward people like us on many levels. Such arrogance is expressed within the financing assumptions of the system that cannot reach an understanding about how to make health care both widespread and solvent. It extends to denying us worth in exchange for deference. It embraces even those of us who run away from any idea that we deserve to feel good about ourselves and our futures.

To change the assumptions about us to make us well is to make us the center of the assumptions. Whatever system works for us works *because* of us -- not despite us. The world in which that system works exists with us at the center -- not just allowed to come in by the back door.

The consequence of that shift in assumptions is the assumption of our worth. If we cannot assume and articulate our own value, we can expect no one else to do so for us.

Finally, that shift in assumptions anticipates yet another dislocation: our acceptance of what it means to have us in charge. Such change means a system that not only works for Black folk, but a system in which the Black folk do the work.

We are the actuaries who structure the economic models for the insurers who underwrite the care. We are the care givers. We are the administrators. We are the ultimate underwriters. We are the educators of both the participants and the care givers. We are the caretakers of the values and assumptions of our own health maintenance. Only in these circumstances then does care and treatment translate into independence. Only within these circumstances does compassion not breed hopelessness and helplessness.

The New Vision

We start with the objective of nourishing people in their strength and independence -- not their infirmity. We focus our understanding of health on promoting wellness by empowering people to prevent illness. In this way, our community model must embrace all of us within its resources to create for us a nurturing cocoon that not only relieves our pain but secures our well-being

The model is not a hospital model. It is a community model that requires the involvement of an entire community to finance the framework, to empower those within it to generate the values that make it work, and to provide the structure that accords the care to make people healthy.

We look to changing the choices people make about how they live their lives. The resources this effort creates we allocate to those institutions that affect and influence the changed thinking and conduct on which the effort depends.

We also look to aggregating our health care dollars to form a new power block. In this way, we can demonstrate the economic value of Black folk and influence the decisions of others within the health care framework to make decisions that satisfy our interests, as we define them.

Where care is required, we require structures that afford compassion, without disempowering the people we intend to help with our care. To do this, we require a system that empowers and authorizes people like those that the system otherwise would be compassionate toward.

Finally, we must change what we expect from the system. We must settle upon an understanding of health that makes a difference in the lives of Black folk. Much of what ails us is not just a breakdown of the body. It is a deterioration of the spirit.

That deterioration reflects the ills of our world in which we may not know the joy of achieving as we would choose. It is a world in which we may not receive the reward of our worth or feel the safety and security of a home in which we are at its center.

In many ways, we must reinvent what health means to have meaning for people like us. For us, health may not only mean doctors and nurses and pharmacists. It also means markets, community, friendship and family, and future.

For us, these issues of economics, education, housing and community are directly related to our health. Within these issues are the barriers that separate us not just from getting by to prosperity, but also from just not feeling bad to feeling good.

Afterthoughts:
Weaving a New Fabric of Community

We end our New Thinking only by beginning again. The thinking never ends. The questioning continues. The only certainty that our searching brings is the certainty that the best answer to a hard question is yet another question.

In proceeding as we have, we hope to have accomplished nothing other than to spark an inquiry among people like us about what it means for people like us to prosper together on this continent. We have, as the focus of our discussion, thoughts about housing, economic development, education, and health care -- all for Black folk. Yet, the real subject of our new thinking is the meaning of *community*.

We use the word to mean many things. It is the place we find ourselves or run away from to escape ourselves. It is shorthand for the collective reference to people who look like us. It is the repository of what we value. It is the embodiment of what we fear, what little we have, what much we need, what limits we endure, or what frightens our oppressor. Not often enough, it stands for what we can become.

More than a place, community is an idea. Ideas are powerful things, particularly when they are fueled by thought. When they are fueled by the thought of the people who think and conceive them, an idea makes the thinking person powerful. That power of such thinking also makes the thinker free.

These discussions, therefore, give substance to the slogan "Power to the People" by making the idea of *community* an instrument of the imagination of people like us. In our imaginations, the community can be whatever we choose it to be. It takes whatever shape we command of it.

Yet, thought demands one additional thing of us. We must understand how the community that prospers in our imagination can also work in the real world. Certainly, once we can concretely conceive of what prosperity for us must mean, it is a simpler next step to follow the idea to its realization. We do this, too, only by thinking.

New Thinking invites more thinking, not to indulge in an intellectual exercise, but to inform action to transform our world to work for us.

At the center of this new world is the community. Time after time in our discussions, we have returned to the community. It has served as the setting for housing that transforms a development of brick and mortar into a neighborhood of rising people. It has served as the market for our economy of human capital. It has served as a venue of learning that fires the imaginations that give us power and create value for us. Last, it is the home that nurtures us and keeps us safe and well.

In shaping this public policy by African Americans for African Americans, community provides the foundation. Wherever we come out in our policy choices, we necessarily fashion this idea we call *community*. In fashioning this policy that works for us, we had better be sure that the community our policy supports is one we would want to live in. While the choices we make about how we think can make us free, these same choices have consistently ensnared us -- particularly when the thinking behind the choices was not our own.

The point of New Thinking is to engage everyday people in the important decisions that shape the world in which they live. We require no special position to engage in such thinking. We need no wealth to pursue our dreams. We need no special office just to say what is or is not acceptable to us. We simply take this freedom by exercising it.

We invite you to think about these notions we have outlined here on your own. We implore you to ask your own questions and explore your own answers. The only magic in what you think is that the thinking is yours.

Appendix: Extending New Thinking
A New Thinking Primer

There is no trick to New Thinking. It is just listening, thinking, questioning, more thinking, sharing, thinking again, and then bringing it all together to question some more.

What are we thinking about? Just simply what we want the world to be; what our small piece of it must look like to produce the results we want; and, most importantly, what each of us need do to make our vision real.

We invite you to question and think about what you read here, alone in the solitude of your private thoughts and together with others in the hothouse of your discussions with family, friends, and neighbors. The power of New Thinking is not your agreement with us or with your friends. Rather, it is in the power of your thinking together to produce something that not one of you ever thought to consider.

That was our surprising experience. We lay out for you here what we did, not as a manual for you to follow, but as an example to get you started.

We began for ordinary reasons. We wanted to get together with others like us to share the comfort of familiarity that many of us had so little chance to enjoy. In the comfort that familiarity brought, we challenged ourselves to make a different outcome for African Americans than we often saw.

We began with ten of us. What brought us together was our common tie with one member of the group and our common interest in people like us.

CLAIRVOYANCE

We began by having dinner. We met each month for dinner together to solve the world's problems. We have been meeting each month now for more than four years.

Over the course of those years, we discussed articles, papers, issues, and concerns. We developed those four ground rules for our discussions earlier set forth:

1. Leave your egos at the door.
2. Leave your agendas at the door.
3. Confidentiality is sacrosanct.
4. Be prepared to challenge your own assumptions.

Within these rules, we learned to trust and respect one another. As we did not always agree, we always discussed and questioned. Where that led was not compromise, but *synthesis*. The product of our probing was not just a little of this idea or a little of that idea, but an entirely different idea -- usually a more exciting and intriguing idea than the ones we initially debated.

Our aim was not just good conversation. We wanted to affect things around us for people like us. On one occasion, when an African American leader in our city was under attack for taking actions that seemed to us plainly to be in the interests of Black folk, we sought to help.

As we explored what we might do, we considered a variety of things that people had done before. We thought about holding an event to honor the official, having a press conference to show support, or writing letters to the newspaper that had been the source of the attacks.

As we thought and questioned more, we reached several conclusions. First, the attacks that concerned us reflected a view of things that we did not share and believed that other African Americans might not share as well. Second, in our town, the interests and viewpoints of African Americans were not very clearly expressed as different from those prevailing in the general population. Finally, the outcome of policy issues framed by the mainstream of thought might not be the same as the outcome of those same policies framed by African Americans asserting themselves plainly as African Americans.

As we pondered, we concluded that we could serve the leadership of our community more long term by encouraging to emerge a body of thinking unashamedly Black than by holding press conferences. We then proceeded to hold a number of small forums among ourselves, outside of the public glare, for that body of thought to come together.

A small group of us proceeded as was described in **An Overview of New Thinking**. We first identified the issues we thought warranted our attention and laid out how we would approach them.

Our interest was not paralleling the policy debates that surrounded us. We sought to frame the debate in a way that produced a constructive result for African Americans. We, therefore, chose what we saw as a "community building" agenda, looking at housing, economic development, education, health care, transportation, and raising the next generation.

Of course, the popular focus was on crime, drugs, teen pregnancy or other elements of the pathologies around us that seemed to command so much of the public's attention. Our view was that, if we succeeded in resolving the issues we chose to consider and created the kind of community that we believed we all deserved, these other problems would cease to be problems or would be resolved as we addressed *our* issues.

We also decided that the point of getting together was thought and discussion, as we had enjoyed with our monthly dinners. When we considered who to include in our expanded discussions, we looked to people first who would be comfortable with discussion under our ground rules than who would have some special knowledge to add to the discussion. For that special knowledge to make a difference to us, it would have to be communicated in a way that would provoke us to think. Absent such provocation of our thinking, special knowledge had limited value in and of itself.

As we saw the issues we were probing, we began with the premise that there were no experts. Had there been, then there would be no reason for us to consider the issues we were considering, as the problems would have been solved already. Second, we considered that, for our solution to work, we would all have to be experts, because solving these problems would have to engage all of us. No one could afford to sit by waiting for someone else to lend his or her expertise to our aid.

In all, we have held five sessions, each one involving any-where from 25 to more than 35 participants. A little more than 100 persons have attended at least one of the five sessions.

In inviting each of the people, one member of our group spoke personally with the participant. He shared with everyone who had contributed time to join with us our experience in talking with one another, the ground rules, and the good results that our talking together had produced.

In beginning New Thinking, the fundamental question for us was "what do we want for ourselves?" From there, we asked "what then does it mean for us to make a desired outcome a reality?" What do we have to do, and what do we have to bring about? To answer these questions, we had to probe honestly about ourselves and about many things we now assume. To change an outcome, we proceeded then to consider how we must change ourselves and the assumptions we, and others, have about the world.

Taking these thoughts into account, we suggest the following considerations for your discussions:

1. **Come together as friends.** On the surface, it may seem that having a group of people representative of a cross-section of the community might be more desirable or that a gathering of people with special knowledge might be more productive. However, these considerations miss the point of New Thinking: conversation to identify and challenge other-wise unstated assumptions and rework the assumptions to suit better the interests of people like the folks in the room. The process of challenging assumptions and questioning premises is often hard on relationships. To do it well, New Thinking requires respect and trust. These elements are most present when the participants start off in a relationship where these elements are key.

2. **Be ready to question, but not to dismiss.** New Thinking is not debating. No one wins in New Thinking by being right. The group wins only when questioning and probing produce a better thought no individual considered before. Bad ideas, too, are important to New Thinking if questioning discloses *why* the idea is bad. New Thinking has no use for even a good idea, unless *why* the idea is good is articulated and understood. It is from understanding why this idea is good or that one is bad that the next new idea emerges from the discussion.

3. **Don't fall in love with your own position or be too anxious to disagree.** New Thinking requires patience. The thought is not complete until you follow its consequences to the ultimate conclusion. Thoughts stated incompletely may appear to be in conflict. However, when you follow the course of the reasoning or probe the underlying assumptions, you might find that the positions inevitably converge.

4. **If you find yourself disagreeing with another, assume that there is a rational basis for the disagreement and work to understand what that disagreement ultimately means.** That someone should dare disagree with you may not reflect the other person's pig-headedness, stupidity, or timidity. It may be that the other persons knows facts that you do not or is proceeding under a different set of assumptions than you are. It will help both of you to understand better the issue on which you disagree by identifying the

conflicts in facts and possibly conflicting assumptions. When you together work out these conflicts, you may discover yet another position both of you may favor together even more than the initial positions you took separately.

5. **Synthesis is not tossed salad.** New Thinking is not a hodgepodge of views. It is not New Thinking to come together, share viewpoints, take something from one person and put it together with something else from another person in order to come up with an amalgam on which everyone can agree. Rather, New Thinking requires analysis. You have to identify, understand, and choose the working assumptions on which the group agrees. You must also identify the understood facts on which the group agrees or decide how to find the facts the group may need to answer its questions. Then, with understood assumptions and openly stated facts, the group can reason and reach a rational conclusion that may be a position earlier stated or something different altogether. In either case, the group will be able to explain what it is talking about and why it desires a particular outcome.

6. **Keep the discussion simple.** We often forget that the essence of genius is to simplify the complicated. That is because people of genius deal with the complex by breaking it down to, or building it up from, simple components. Get in the habit of talking, using simple terms, vivid images, and illustrative stories rather than high sounding concepts that

others may not understand the same as you. Relying upon such concepts stated in jargon, the group may believe it has agreement when the individuals may understand the terms of discussion differently. Or, the group may struggle for the longest time in disagreement over questions of semantics. Clear discussion, full of examples, images, and anecdotes, avoids unnecessary disagreement or a false sense of agreement when further discussion is warranted.

7. **Every policy question is personal.** With the increasing complexity of policy discussions we see and hear around us, we forget one undying fact: all policy is ultimately personal. Whatever gets decided, we have to live with it. The discussion is never academic. The basic policy question is inevitably a personal one: "What do I want to see happen?" The answer to that question does not require great learning or special knowledge. It requires only that we be honest with ourselves enough to say what we want and patient enough to probe why we want it. In New Thinking, the point is to make clear and understandable our personal vision to others who have their own personal vision, in order to find and shape a vision all of us can share and work to achieve.

8. **Information is a tool, not an end in itself.** Sometimes the sheer volume of information before us simply makes us stop thinking so we can just manage to comprehend it all. New Thinking is about assumptions and outcomes. What we decide our assumptions should be will decide what informa-

tion we need to know. We don't need to master any outside information to know what we want to happen. We just need to think about it and then say it clearly and in plain terms so that we cannot be misunderstood.

9. **Listen and wait.** Not everyone needs to hear the wonderful ideas we happen to have. However, we benefit hearing what others have to say that we never considered.

10. **If you cannot break out of the past and the present, try circling back from the future.** In whichever time we find ourselves, we are likely to view the problems of our time to be more challenging before we solve them than we would find them just after we had figured out how to solve them. Our policy discussions inevitably will focus us on a present with problems that seem so imposing and of such long standing that we hardly believe mortals such as we can solve them. However, things may look less difficult from a future that has already taken care of these concerns. Just imagine what that future looks like -- and then work backwards to discover how these people, just like us, solved the problems that now beset us.

The above considerations are just a few of the things we did to sustain our discussions to find answers we had not before considered. You may find these suggestions helpful.

It may also be helpful to keep your discussion groups manageably small, to allow for the most informal conversation involving the greatest number of people sharing their ideas. If you have a large group of people, rather than have one big discussion group, have several smaller, more intimate groups.

We found that in larger groups, some participants shied away from discussion while a few bolder souls dominated the conversation. We found that we thought more, and more creatively, without the audience of some listening while others put forth.

To generate the kind of trust that New Thinking requires, you should think about supporting a small core group of people who meet on a regular basis. This core group can give to new comers a sense of the ground rules by how these established participants conduct themselves. With such a core group, the intimacy of the group will be sufficiently appealing that new comers may more readily submit themselves to the process.

We found that, from time to time, we were on the verge of disagreements that we thought we could not bridge or at such a silence that we might say nothing of value. At those times, we were tempted to manipulate the discussion to force some resolution.

However, at those times of apparent anxiety, we could only trust in the process to take us beyond the point of difficulty. Time and time again, the process did just that. By trusting in the process, we were just trusting in one another. That trust in one another lies at the heart of New Thinking.

New Thinking Continues . . .

If you liked what you read -- or you didn't like it, but it made you think -- pass it on. Share **Clairvoyance** with your family, your neighbors, and your friends.

If you'd like to order more copies of **Clairvoyance**, use the form two pages ahead to order more copies direct from New Thinking Publications.

If you have thoughts to share, an idea to offer, or just a bone to pick, write to us at the address below:

New Thinking Publications
c/o Associated Black Charities
1114 Cathedral Street
Baltimore, Maryland 21201
e-mail: abcbalto@clark.net

Or, e-mail John H. Morris, Jr. directly at

jmorris706@aol.com.

We want to extend the thinking beyond us, and beyond you.

More Clairvoyance Ahead

In the months ahead, New Thinking Publications would like to follow up on **Clairvoyance** with

- **More New Thinking** on the following topics:
  Transportation
  Raising the Next Generation
  More Thinking on **Clairvoyance**: Addressing New Issues

- New Thinking Publications is also considering a book devoted entirely to Sylvia. Look for **The Sylvia Chronicle: *Sketches in the Life of a Woman Who Learned She Could Grab the Future by the Neck.***
  It continues the account of how Sylvia managed to take over the Hospital, how Baka started his enterprise, and the future of DuBois Village with Sylvia, Sara, Baka, and the rest of the Village.

- Finally, to help you with your New Thinking, New Thinking Publications is also seeking to compile materials for a New Thinking Kit, to give you more of the benefit of our experiences as you seek to question and challenge old assumptions.

For more information, write to New Thinking Publications.

ORDER Clairvoyance TODAY. Complete this form. Enclose your check made payable to "New Thinking Publications", and mail it back to New Thinking Publications, c/o Associated Black Charities, 1114 Cathedral Street, Baltimore, Maryland 21201, or call at (410) 659-0000.

Name: _____

Street Address: _____

City: _____ State: _____

Zip Code: _____

Number of Books Ordered: _____   x $19.95 $ _____

*Shipping (optional — if desired)
For up to 3 books   2.24

Total Enclosed $ _____

* Ordered books available directly at ABC for pick up. Call ABC for cost of shipping more than 3 books ordered.